A Sharper Choice on North Korea

Engaging China for a Stable Northeast Asia

D1411622

COUNCIL *on*
FOREIGN
RELATIONS

Independent Task Force Report No. 74

Mike Mullen and
Sam Nunn, *Chairs*
Adam Mount, *Project Director*

A Sharper Choice
on North Korea
Engaging China for a Stable Northeast Asia

The Council on Foreign Relations (CFR) is an independent, nonpartisan membership organization, think tank, and publisher dedicated to being a resource for its members, government officials, business executives, journalists, educators and students, civic and religious leaders, and other interested citizens in order to help them better understand the world and the foreign policy choices facing the United States and other countries. Founded in 1921, CFR carries out its mission by maintaining a diverse membership, with special programs to promote interest and develop expertise in the next generation of foreign policy leaders; convening meetings at its headquarters in New York and in Washington, DC, and other cities where senior government officials, members of Congress, global leaders, and prominent thinkers come together with CFR members to discuss and debate major international issues; supporting a Studies Program that fosters independent research, enabling CFR scholars to produce articles, reports, and books and hold roundtables that analyze foreign policy issues and make concrete policy recommendations; publishing *Foreign Affairs*, the preeminent journal on international affairs and U.S. foreign policy; sponsoring Independent Task Forces that produce reports with both findings and policy prescriptions on the most important foreign policy topics; and providing up-to-date information and analysis about world events and American foreign policy on its website, www.cfr.org.

The Council on Foreign Relations takes no institutional positions on policy issues and has no affiliation with the U.S. government. All views expressed in its publications and on its website are the sole responsibility of the author or authors.

The Council on Foreign Relations sponsors Independent Task Forces to assess issues of current and critical importance to U.S. foreign policy and provide policymakers with concrete judgments and recommendations. Diverse in backgrounds and perspectives, Task Force members aim to reach a meaningful consensus on policy through private deliberations. Once launched, Task Forces are independent of CFR and solely responsible for the content of their reports. Task Force members are asked to join a consensus signifying that they endorse "the general policy thrust and judgments reached by the group, though not necessarily every finding and recommendation." Each Task Force member also has the option of putting forward an additional or dissenting view. Members' affiliations are listed for identification purposes only and do not imply institutional endorsement. Task Force observers participate in discussions, but are not asked to join the consensus.

For further information about CFR or this Task Force, please write to the Council on Foreign Relations, 58 East 68th Street, New York, NY 10065, or call the Communications office at 212.434.9888. Visit CFR's website at www.cfr.org.

This report is printed on paper that is FSC® Chain-of-Custody Certified by a printer who is certified by BM TRADA North America Inc.

Task Force Members

Task Force members are asked to join a consensus signifying that they endorse "the general policy thrust and judgments reached by the group, though not necessarily every finding and recommendation." They participate in the Task Force in their individual, not institutional, capacities.

Victor D. Cha*
Georgetown University

Roberta Cohen
Committee for Human Rights in North Korea

Joseph R. DeTrani
Daniel Morgan Academy

Nicholas Eberstadt*
American Enterprise Institute

Robert J. Einhorn
Brookings Institution

Bonnie S. Glaser*
Center for Strategic and International Studies

Mary Beth Long*
Foundation for Defense of Democracies

Catherine B. Lotrionte
Georgetown University

Evan S. Medeiros*
Eurasia Group

Adam Mount
Center for American Progress

Mike Mullen
MGM Consulting, LLC

Sam Nunn
Nuclear Threat Initiative

Gary Samore
Harvard University

Walter L. Sharp*
Sharp Advice, LLC

Mitchel B. Wallerstein*
Baruch College

Robert F. Willard
Institute of Nuclear Power Operations

Juan Carlos Zarate
Financial Integrity Network, LLC

*The individual has endorsed the report and signed an additional or dissenting view.

*This report is dedicated to Ambassador Stephen Bosworth,
a respected diplomat and scholar who worked tirelessly
for a peaceful resolution of the North Korea nuclear issue
and inspired others to do the same.*

Contents

Foreword

North Korea poses a grave and growing threat to the United States and its allies. The regime's development of new conventional, missile, and nuclear capabilities puts civilians of allied countries, U.S. military personnel, and the American people in real danger. North Korea has reached this point as a result of sustained Chinese support (or at least acquiescence), along with a series of decisions by U.S. policymakers over the decades not to take military action to prevent the regime from attaining or maintaining a nuclear capability.

The year 2016 has been turbulent on the Korean Peninsula, but the underlying trends remain unchanged. North Korea has carried out a series of nuclear and missile tests. The regime continues to pose a conventional military threat to the Republic of Korea while committing crimes against humanity against its own citizens. China for its part continues to shield the regime from international pressure and to provide it with support that enables its illegal and dangerous behavior. The United States has succeeded in winning new sanctions authority, but enforcement has been slow and is highly unlikely to change Pyongyang's behavior in meaningful ways. Without a shift in U.S. strategy toward North Korea, the next U.S. president will likely be sitting in the Oval Office when the regime finally acquires the ability to strike the continental United States with a nuclear weapon.

This growing threat has impelled the Council on Foreign Relations to again convene an Independent Task Force to assess the state of U.S. policy toward North Korea and to propose a new strategy. The report reaches the landmark conclusion that current trends will increasingly threaten the United States and its allies, in particular the Republic of Korea and Japan. It is therefore not enough to maintain the status quo on the peninsula or to wait for circumstances to evolve in a favorable way. The Task Force proposes new ideas to expand regional dialogue, restructure negotiations, protect the human rights of North Korea's citizens, strictly enforce new sanctions authority, and deter and defend against a regime that poses a steadily increasing threat. This strategy would create or expand critical instruments for changing China's behavior, including a regional mechanism for enforcing new sanctions authority, a new effort to pressure North Korea on human rights through the United Nations system, and new military steps to bolster deterrence and offset North Korea's missile capabilities. The next administration should consider each recommendation carefully.

Recognizing that Chinese pressure could have a decisive effect on Pyongyang, the Task Force recommends that U.S. officials undertake a major diplomatic effort to elevate the issue to the top of the U.S.-China bilateral relationship and enlist China in bringing about a stable and nonnuclear Korean Peninsula. If the United States does so and the Chinese government declines to go along, it would raise serious questions as to China's willingness to be a responsible regional and global actor. It would also necessitate that the United States consult closely with both South Korea and Japan and consider adopting a new strategic posture, one that did not rule out military options against a nuclear-armed North Korea with global reach.

I thank the chairs of this Task Force, Mike Mullen and Sam Nunn, as well as its individual members and observers for lending their experience, judgment, and creativity to this urgent task. Their broad expertise inside and outside of government helped to create a practical and powerful document. My thanks extend also to CFR's Task Force Program Director Anya Schmemann and her predecessor, Chris Tuttle, for shaping the endeavor and also to Project Director Adam Mount for ably guiding the group and drafting this important report. The determination of all involved to produce a substantive and consequential set of findings and recommendations speaks to the severity and urgency of the threat. They have provided ideas; the next administration should consider them carefully and modify U.S. policy accordingly.

Richard N. Haass
President
Council on Foreign Relations
September 2016

Acknowledgments

In many ways, North Korea is unique among nations. Its rejection of the international standards of stability, development, and justice threatens not only the people of Northeast Asia but also the moral structure on which global order is built. This Task Force on North Korea comes at a critical time for U.S. policy. The next administration will inherit a foreign policy that is pulled between competing crises that collectively conspire to unravel the U.S. rebalance to Asia. It will not be easy to devote scarce time and attention to an issue marked by inertia, frustration, and limited options. However, the security of U.S. allies and the future order of maritime Asia demand that the next president place North Korea at the top of the agenda. The proposals contained in this report are an attempt to catalyze new debate on North Korea and provide new options for the next presidential administration. They are the result of a great deal of effort from the distinguished participants of this Task Force as well as several external advisors.

The project's two chairs, Admiral Mike Mullen and Senator Sam Nunn, have guided and motivated this endeavor at every step. Their judgment, experience, and ardent conviction of the need to produce an innovative report have pushed the entire group to reconsider our preconceptions about this difficult issue. At the same time, their patience, generosity, and humor have made the process a pleasure. I am also grateful to their staffs, including Mack Alston at MGM Consulting, LLC, and Tempe Stephen at the Nuclear Threat Initiative, who helped to coordinate busy schedules and the frequent exchange of materials.

The Task Force is fortunate to have been composed of exceptionally experienced, diligent, and constructive members. It is customary at this point to recognize members who made an unusual contribution to a report, but, in fact, each member at various times made a decisive contribution to this report, and nearly all submitted multiple rounds of detailed comments on drafts. It has been a privilege and a pleasure to work with each of them.

Thanks are also due to a number of external experts who were gracious enough to share data and discuss their perspectives, including James Acton, Andrea Berger, Kurt Campbell, Darcie Draudt, Mark Fitzpatrick, Michael Fuchs, Van Jackson, Choi Kang, Andrei Lankov, Mira Rapp-Hooper, and a group of human rights experts organized by Task Force member Roberta Cohen. Several officials from both the U.S. and South Korean governments also shared their time and knowledge; I am convinced that the time and consideration they have invested in the alliance over the past decade has left it in a strong position to navigate the difficult years ahead. None of them bears responsibility for the content of the report.

The report also benefitted from two meetings of CFR members who met to discuss the rapidly evolving events in North Korea and provide input for the project. Task Force members Gary Samore and Victor Cha joined me at roundtables in New York and in Washington, respectively. I am grateful to them, the CFR members who attended to lend their advice, and to CFR's New York and Washington Meetings teams for facilitating the events.

My gratitude extends to CFR's Publications team for editing and readying the report for publication, as well as to Lisa Ortiz of CFR Digital and Josh Linden of GoodFolk, who helped produce the graphics within this report. My thanks to CFR's Communications, Corporate, Digital, National, Outreach, and Washington External Affairs teams for enabling the report to reach the widest possible audience.

Anya Schmemann and Veronica Chiu of CFR's Independent Task Force Program were instrumental in managing the process and providing valuable advice on both the content and form of the report. I am also grateful to my research associate Theresa Lou, program associate Chelie Setzer, and interns Erin Sielaff and Adriana Guardans-Godo for exemplary research support and editorial advice. Chris Tuttle, former managing director of CFR's Task Force program, deserves special recognition for initiating this important study at a critical time and for assembling the group. My colleagues at CFR, Senior Fellows Janine Davidson (since departed from CFR), Sheila Smith, Paul Stares, and Stewart Patrick also provided valuable advice. In addition, Scott Snyder provided consistent guidance on the process from start to finish and involved me in several interesting CFR roundtables.

I am also grateful to several people and organizations who have supported my other work while I undertook this project and made allowances for my involvement: CFR Senior Vice President and Director of Studies James M. Lindsay and Director of Studies Administration Amy Baker, the National Security and International Policy Program at the Center for American Progress (CAP), led by CAP Vice President Vikram Singh and Managing Director Nathan Fenstermacher, and the Ploughshares Fund.

CFR President Richard Haass has supported, guided, and advised this endeavor from the beginning. Last, Ambassador Stephen Bosworth served as the initial co-chair of this Task Force and helped frame our effort and assemble our outstanding group. This report is dedicated to his memory.

Adam Mount
Project Director

Acronyms

COI	commission of inquiry
CVID	complete, verifiable, and irreversible denuclearization
DMZ	demilitarized zone
DPRK	Democratic People's Republic of Korea
IAEA	International Atomic Energy Agency
ICBM	intercontinental ballistic missile
MLRS	multiple launch rocket artillery system
NATO	North Atlantic Treaty Organization
NGO	nongovernmental organization
ROK	Republic of Korea
SOF	Special Operations forces
THAAD	Terminal High-Altitude Area Defense
UN	United Nations

Map

NORTH KOREA AND SELECT MISSILE TEST LOCATIONS*

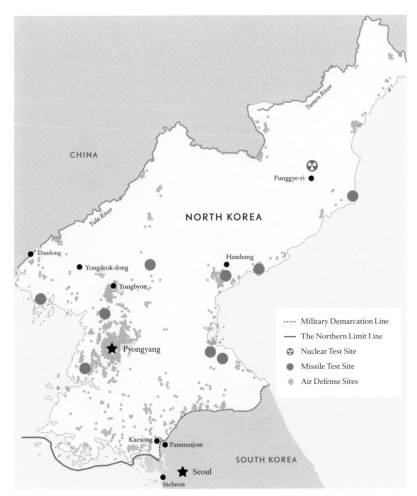

*Air defense sites current as of June 25, 2009.

Source: North Korean Economy Watch, "North Korea Uncovered," 2009.

Independent Task Force Report

Executive Summary

Since 1953, when an armistice put an end to the major military operations of the Korean War, the Democratic People's Republic of Korea (DPRK), the Republic of Korea (ROK), and the United States Forces Korea have been trapped in an increasingly dangerous cycle in which North Korea provokes a militarized crisis until minor concessions settle the situation at a new normal. The U.S.-ROK alliance has succeeded in preventing these recurrent crises from igniting a war, but this cycle of provocation hides perilous long-term trends. North Korea's accelerating nuclear and missile programs pose a grave and expanding threat to the territory of U.S. allies, to U.S. personnel stationed in the region, and to the continental United States. More generally, North Korea's behavior has endangered the emergence of a stable and prosperous Northeast Asia.

The United States and its allies have failed to meet their critical objectives: to roll back North Korea's expanding nuclear and ballistic missile programs and prevent it from spreading nuclear and missile technology to dangerous actors around the world. China's reluctance to pressure the DPRK has allowed the regime to further destabilize a region critical to U.S. national interests, to systematically perpetrate crimes against humanity, and to threaten the safety of U.S. allies. The countervailing diplomatic, economic, and military steps required to deter and contain the North Korean regime threaten to aggravate U.S. tensions with China just as the United States and its regional partners are attempting to encourage China's rise to remain consistent with a peaceful, prosperous, and just regional order.

Yet developments in the past year have altered the North Korea problem in important ways. In March 2016, the United Nations (UN) Security Council—with China's consent—unanimously passed Resolution 2270 to significantly strengthen the sanctions regime that restricts arms transfers and limits trade with North Korea. Pyongyang's actions and Beijing's reticence have also provided incentive for closer military cooperation between the United States and its allies, including on missile defense. Additionally, South Korean President Park Geun-hye has made concerted efforts to improve the ROK's bilateral relations with both China and Japan, and a new round of regional diplomacy has improved coordination over the North Korean nuclear problem.[1] Yet North Korea is also accelerating the development of a capability to strike the continental United States, as well as U.S. allies, with a nuclear warhead delivered by an intercontinental ballistic missile (ICBM).[2] These developments present the U.S. president with an exigent threat of a North Korea that can strike at the United States—but also with new opportunities to halt the cycle of provocation and prevent North Korea from achieving this capability.

China's policy toward the DPRK will critically affect the fate of the region. If China, the United States, and U.S. allies can work together to pressure North Korea to abandon its nuclear program and mitigate its threatening military posture, a stable, prosperous Northeast Asia led by China and U.S. allies can emerge; if they cannot, the DPRK's recklessness will further strain the U.S.-China relationship and destabilize a region vital to both countries' interests. For this reason, encouraging a transformation of China's policy toward North Korea should be the next administration's top priority in its relations with China. This transformation should be accomplished through a sequence of steps to gradually increase the pressure on China to support a cooperative approach, which could result in the peaceful resolution of the armistice, the elimination of nuclear capability, and the eventual reunification of the Korean Peninsula.

In this context, the Council on Foreign Relations convened an Independent Task Force on U.S. Policy Toward North Korea to assess the efficacy of existing policy and offer recommendations to U.S. policymakers on reducing the threat from North Korea for the remainder of President Barack Obama's presidency, as well as for the next administration. The Task Force assesses that the current policy of strategic patience will not halt the recurrent and dangerous cycle of provocation or ensure a stable regional security order into the future. If allowed to continue, current trends will predictably, progressively, and gravely threaten U.S. national security interests and those of its allies.

Halting these alarming and negative trends requires a new strategy toward North Korea and the region, one guided by a broader organizing principle: to bring about a stable and prosperous Northeast Asia that U.S. allies have a hand in leading. In the long run, achieving this vision requires that the Korean Peninsula be free of nuclear weapons and respectful of human rights, whether by genuine transformation of the North Korean regime or by unification. U.S. policy toward North Korea will have to be integrated with broader U.S. strategy for maritime Asia, or both are likely to fail.

The United States should present North Korea with a sharper choice: seek a negotiated settlement to return to compliance with UN resolutions on nuclear weapons or face severe and escalating costs. These steps should be carefully and deliberately sequenced to calibrate pressure on North Korea—to credibly signal to Pyongyang that the United States and its allies will continually increase pressure until serious talks resume, to ensure that the regime has an opportunity to respond to specific pressure tactics at designated junctures, and to maximize opportunities to work with China.

The United States should act immediately to secure its interests and those of its allies against the grave and growing North Korean nuclear and missile threats by expanding U.S.-ROK-Japan cooperation to actively and strictly enforce sanctions on North Korea and by strengthening its joint deterrence profile.

On a parallel course, the United States and its allies should offer restructured negotiations that provide genuine incentives for North Korea to participate in substantive talks while increasing pressure by strictly enforcing the new sanctions in UN Security Council Resolution 2270, targeting North Korean illicit activity, and encouraging other nations in the region—including China—to join this effort. If Pyongyang refuses this proposal, the United States should seek new multilateral sanctions to restrict the regime's funding sources and enact additional military measures to strengthen allied deterrence of military attacks. New nuclear tests or military attacks by North Korea should accelerate this timetable. North Korea should not be allowed to use talks as a way of detracting attention from bad behavior, as has been the case in the past. Abrogation of the testing ban, new attacks, or stalled talks should result in their termination.

The United States should also make a new approach to China. To enlist China in the effort to bring about a stable and nonnuclear Korean Peninsula, U.S. officials should propose a dialogue on the future of the Korean Peninsula to demonstrate that it is in both countries' security interests to find a comprehensive resolution to the problem. A unified response to North Korea stands the greatest chance of finding a lasting solution on the peninsula and of forging a stable and prosperous Northeast Asia, and is by far the preferable course of action.

As long as North Korea retains a nuclear capability, the U.S.-China relationship will be strained. To the extent that Beijing declines to cooperate or this effort does not show results, the United States and its allies will have no choice but to greatly accelerate efforts with Japan and South Korea to bring about a Korean Peninsula without nuclear weapons.

FINDINGS AND RECOMMENDATIONS

The Task Force reached ten findings and six recommendations. These support five broad principles for U.S. policy: promote a stable and prosperous Northeast Asia, restructure negotiations, protect human rights, enforce sanctions and escalate financial pressure, and strengthen deterrence and defense.

Finding

1. In its assessment of the status of the North Korean regime, the Task Force finds that North Korean leader Kim Jong-un has ruthlessly consolidated power and there is low probability of regime collapse in the near future. Over time, however, North Korean citizens' increasing access to information from the outside world, as well as growing internal markets, could form the basis for a gradual transformation of the totalitarian system.

PROMOTE A STABLE AND PROSPEROUS NORTHEAST ASIA

Findings

2. The Task Force finds that although China remains North Korea's primary patron, it is increasingly willing to exert pressure to curb the regime's erratic behavior.

3. The Task Force finds that South Korea's improving relations with Japan and China present new opportunities for cooperation on North Korea policy.

4. The Task Force finds that South Korea can be an effective representative of shared U.S.-ROK interests, including deterrence signaling to North Korea, coordination with China, and regional diplomacy to promote sanctions enforcement.

Recommendations

I. To ensure that U.S. policy remains consistent with the long-term objective of a stable and prosperous Northeast Asia, the Task Force recommends that the United States and its allies engage China as soon as possible to plan for the future of the Korean Peninsula. These talks, both trilateral and in a five-party format, should plan for militarized crises, collapse scenarios, and the role of a unified Korea in Northeast Asian security.

- Five-party talks consisting of China, Japan, Russia, South Korea, and the United States should begin as soon as possible to prepare a common proposal for the next round of multilateral negotiations and also to discuss other areas of regional concern. In this way, the parties can accomplish the intended regional stability functions of the Six Party Talks and help promote their resumption.

- To convince China to participate, Washington and Seoul should jointly reassure Beijing that Korean unification will not damage its interests. These steps can include guarantees that Chinese investments on the peninsula will remain intact or be compensated, as well as a dialogue to de-conflict plans for border control, refugees, port access, and military operations during collapse scenarios. The United States and South Korea can also jointly present conditions under which the alliance would consider revising the number and disposition of U.S. forces on the peninsula. Although the alliance should continue in any event, attenuation of the threat may allow for a commensurate reduction of U.S. force posture on the peninsula.

RESTRUCTURE NEGOTIATIONS

Finding

5. Although a negotiated agreement on complete and verifiable denuclearization remains a preferable mechanism for resolving the nuclear issue, the Task Force finds that negotiations are unlikely to eliminate North Korea's nuclear or missile capabilities in the near future. Nonetheless, a new diplomatic approach could potentially freeze North Korea's nuclear and missile programs, establish conditions for increasing pressure if North Korea rejects the proposal, and lay the groundwork for eventual rollback of the regime's nuclear capabilities.

Recommendations

II. The Task Force recommends that the United States move quickly to propose restructured negotiations to limit North Korea's nuclear and missile programs and work toward denuclearization and a comprehensive peace agreement.

- Under this model, the United States should undertake talks subject to the following conditions: first, reaffirmation of the principles of the 2005 Joint Statement, including a nonnuclear peninsula, by all parties; second, progressive steps on the nuclear issue at each stage in the negotiations; third, a moratorium on tests of nuclear weapons and missiles with a range-payload capability greater than existing Scud missiles. The United States and the other members of the talks should avow that they will never accept the DPRK as a nuclear state.

- Early stages of the negotiations should focus on attaining a verified freeze on the DPRK's nuclear capabilities. Additionally, the parties may explore steps on conventional arms control (including limits to the deployment of and exercises with conventional forces), limitations on missile development, nonproliferation of nuclear material or technology, or site-specific inspection of North Korean nuclear facilities.

- The eventual outcome of the talks is a comprehensive deal in which North Korea, South Korea, and the United States, supported by China, sign a peace agreement that will finally end the Korean War and gradually normalize relations in exchange for complete nuclear disarmament and progress on human rights.

PROTECT HUMAN RIGHTS

Finding

6. The Task Force finds that the North Korean state continues to commit grave crimes against humanity, but may be sensitive to international pressure to live up to UN standards on human rights.

Recommendations

III. The Task Force recommends that the United States work with allies, nongovernmental organizations (NGOs), and the United Nations system to escalate pressure on North Korea to respect the human rights of its citizens.

- As a first step, U.S. diplomats should work with global partners to signal that they will move to suspend North Korea's credentials at the United Nations if it does not demonstrate real progress on human rights. To avert this action, North Korea would have to accept visits from UN human rights officials to demonstrate progress. When it meets at the start of each General Assembly session, the UN Credentials Committee can assess whether North Korea has met the requirements.

- U.S. policymakers should facilitate governmental and nongovernmental efforts to allow information about the outside world to reach the North Korean people.

- The United States should support international efforts to seek accountability for North Korean individuals and entities responsible for crimes against humanity while expanding U.S. sanctions against them.

ENFORCE SANCTIONS AND ESCALATE FINANCIAL PRESSURE

Finding

7. The Task Force finds that the recent expansion of the sanctions regime is a necessary step in exerting pressure on North Korea. However, expanded and sustained efforts are required to ensure that they are rigorously implemented and have the desired effects, including measures to provide amenable states with material assistance and to pressure those that illegally trade with or finance North Korea.

Recommendations

IV. The Task Force recommends that the United States invest in rigorous enforcement of the sanctions regime and apply escalating pressure on North Korea's illicit activities.

- The United States should act quickly to support East and Southeast Asian states in creating a standing multilateral mechanism to coordinate implementation of Resolution 2270. This group should facilitate the sharing of intelligence, coordinate enforcement operations, and distribute resources donated by partners from outside the region, including the United States. Given its sophistication in circumventing previous sanctions, regional states should prioritize interdiction and inspection of North Korean shipping.

- Should North Korea fail to reenter negotiations, the United States should work with its allies to prepare future financial sanctions and other measures that target the full range of the regime's illicit activity, including steps to punish corruption, exporters of slave labor, as well as foreign firms and banks that support these activities, wherever they reside. The United States should allow U.S. companies to bring legal action against sanctions violators and facilitators.

STRENGTHEN DETERRENCE AND DEFENSE

Findings

8. The Task Force finds that North Korea's development of the capability to deliver a nuclear warhead on a long-range ballistic missile would dramatically increase its ability to threaten the United States and its allies.

9. The Task Force finds that although U.S.-ROK deterrence policy may have succeeded in preventing major military attacks since 2010, the frequency and severity of North Korea's aggressive behavior will likely increase as its nuclear and sub-conventional capabilities continue to develop.

Recommendations

V. The Task Force recommends that the United States, South Korea, and Japan move expeditiously to tighten collaboration and strengthen their deterrence and defense posture.

- To reduce North Korea's incentives to divide the three partners with selective military strikes, they should issue a collective security commitment declaring that an attack by North Korea against any one of them is an attack against all.

- The United States, South Korea, and Japan should, through joint exercises and coordinated deployment, expand allied capacity in defensive and offensive cyber operations, antisubmarine capabilities, missile defense, special forces, and air and naval forces to enforce new UN sanctions.

VI. The Task Force recommends that the United States, South Korea, and Japan build capacity to intercept all missile launches with a range-payload capability greater than existing Scud missiles originating from North Korea, whether they are declared to be ballistic missile tests or civil space launch vehicles. In the event that Pyongyang fails to reenter negotiations, or the negotiations fail, the three partners should be prepared to declare and then implement this policy.

Finding

10. The Task Force finds that current trends, if allowed to continue, will predictably, progressively, and gravely threaten U.S. national interests and those of its allies.

This overall strategy seeks to prevent North Korea from attaining the capability to carry out a nuclear strike on the continental United States, but also hedges against the possibility that it does cross this threshold. The proposed enhancements of allied deterrence and defense posture will help ensure that the United States and its allies can meet their national security needs in the years immediately following a successful North Korean test of an ICBM capability. Although it does propose increasing pressure on North Korea to return to the negotiating table, this strategy does not seek to cause the North Korean regime to collapse, an event that is most likely to occur as a result of the regime's continued gross economic mismanagement and cruel and inhumane treatment of its citizens.

However, if North Korea continues to develop its nuclear and long-range missile capabilities and achieves the capability to strike the United States, Washington will have to work with allies to reassess overall strategy toward the regime. That policy review would consider more assertive diplomatic and military steps, including some that directly threaten the regime's nuclear and missile programs and, therefore, the regime itself. At that juncture, these measures may be necessary to protect the United States and its allies and to meet their immutable objective of a stable, free, and nonnuclear Korean Peninsula.

Findings

A CHANGING REGION

Since the end of the Korean War, North Korea has perpetuated a brutal and familiar pattern: the regime carries out a dangerous and often fatal provocation and escalates tensions near to the point of war, following which both sides deescalate the crisis and often agree to talks (figure 1). In August 2015, for example, two South Korean soldiers were maimed by land mines, resulting in a militarized standoff. The Park administration succeeded in extracting a pro forma expression of regret, which led to a brief détente and a reunion of families separated for decades by the Korean War. In late 2015, the Obama administration reportedly made a new attempt to restart negotiations with North Korea but was rebuffed.[3] Six days into the new year, North Korea conducted its fourth nuclear test, which initiated a new round of international condemnation, threats, and sanctions. Tensions remained high through the first half of 2016 as North Korean leader Kim Jong-un threatened military action in response to regular U.S.-ROK spring military exercises and carried out an aggressive program of missile tests.[4]

This 2015 cycle of provocation is the latest iteration of a pattern that has persisted for decades.[5] During this time, the DPRK's diplomatic and economic isolation from the rest of the world has deepened, and only limited information about the outside world reaches North Korean citizens, who continue to struggle with starvation, torture, internment, and execution.

    1. *The Task Force finds that North Korean leader Kim Jong-un has ruthlessly consolidated power and there is low probability of regime collapse in the near future. Over time, however, North Korean citizens' increasing access to information from the outside world, as well as growing internal markets, could form the basis for a gradual transformation of the totalitarian system.*

FIGURE 1: NORTH KOREA'S CYCLES OF PROVOCATION

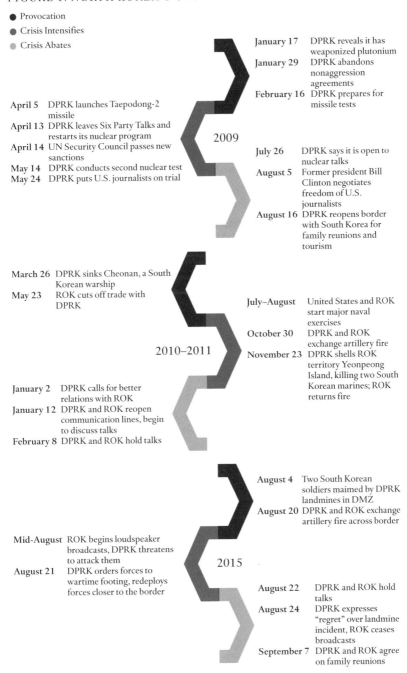

● Provocation
● Crisis Intensifies
● Crisis Abates

2009

January 17 DPRK reveals it has weaponized plutonium
January 29 DPRK abandons nonaggression agreements
February 16 DPRK prepares for missile tests

April 5 DPRK launches Taepodong-2 missile
April 13 DPRK leaves Six Party Talks and restarts its nuclear program
April 14 UN Security Council passes new sanctions
May 14 DPRK conducts second nuclear test
May 24 DPRK puts U.S. journalists on trial

July 26 DPRK says it is open to nuclear talks
August 5 Former president Bill Clinton negotiates freedom of U.S. journalists
August 16 DPRK reopens border with South Korea for family reunions and tourism

2010–2011

March 26 DPRK sinks Cheonan, a South Korean warship
May 23 ROK cuts off trade with DPRK

July–August United States and ROK start major naval exercises
October 30 DPRK and ROK exchange artillery fire
November 23 DPRK shells ROK territory Yeonpeong Island, killing two South Korean marines; ROK returns fire

January 2 DPRK calls for better relations with ROK
January 12 DPRK and ROK reopen communication lines, begin to discuss talks
February 8 DPRK and ROK hold talks

2015

August 4 Two South Korean soldiers maimed by DPRK landmines in DMZ
August 20 DPRK and ROK exchange artillery fire across border

Mid-August ROK begins loudspeaker broadcasts, DPRK threatens to attack them
August 21 DPRK orders forces to wartime footing, redeploys forces closer to the border

August 22 DPRK and ROK hold talks
August 24 DPRK expresses "regret" over landmine incident, ROK ceases broadcasts
September 7 DPRK and ROK agree on family reunions

During North Korea's leadership transitions of 1997 and 2011, when Kim Jong-il assumed power from his father and was then succeeded by his son Kim Jong-un, some in the West predicted that the regime would collapse, scattering refugees and fissile material across the region.[6] In both cases, the regime has endured and succeeded in maintaining centralized authority in Pyongyang. Yet all is not business as usual in North Korea; in 2016, the regime is still struggling to return to normalcy after its new supreme leader initiated a series of gruesome purges that destabilized the ruling elite.[7] The young leader is attempting to revitalize the state's party apparatus as a way of reasserting his control over its leadership. North Korea's economy has largely failed to develop over the last several decades. Pyongyang's centralized control has produced chronic malnutrition, prevailed over a steady decline in imports and exports, and prevented the emergence of a modern industrial or service economy.[8]

At the same time, some facets of daily life in North Korea have seen gradual changes. Under Kim Jong-un, the regime has proved willing to tolerate the emergence of unofficial markets, which, coupled with a brisk cross-border trade with China, has allowed the North Korean economy to grow at marginal rates of 1 to 2 percent, according to some estimates (figure 2).[9] Meanwhile, the regime has become permeable to personal information technology, allowing ordinary citizens access to outside information through foreign DVDs and radio broadcasts and elites to also own USB drives and mobile phones. A recent survey of defectors found that "nearly half the study's sample reported having watched a foreign DVD while in North Korea."[10] Others note the explosion of active mobile phones in the country, which have climbed past two million in a population of twenty-five million (though many of these phones cannot make international calls).[11] Gradual marketization presents opportunities and challenges for U.S. policy. On the one hand, it could widen North Korea's thin middle class and lead to gradual evolution of the regime; on the other, the increasing complexity of its economy affords North Korea greater ability to resist and circumvent the international sanctions regime.

2. *The Task Force finds that although China remains North Korea's primary patron, it is increasingly willing to exert pressure to curb the regime's erratic behavior.*

Even as North Korea continues to revolve through its cycle of provocation and conciliation, changes in the global context and in regional

FIGURE 2: PROPORTION OF NORTH KOREAN BALANCE OF TRADE BY COUNTRY, 1994–2013*

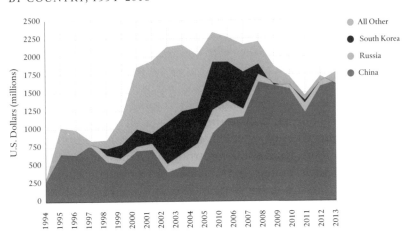

Source: Nicholas Eberstadt, "North Korea's 'Epic Economic Fail' in International Perspective," Asan Institute for Policy Studies, November 2015.

*Unit: 2013 producer-price-index-adjusted illustrative U.S. dollars (millions)

politics present new opportunities to pressure the regime. Despite a long and troubled history, China has continued to serve as a patron of the North Korean regime—as a main trading partner and a defender in the UN Security Council.[12] China's primary interest with respect to North Korea is the maintenance of regional stability: Beijing worries that collapse of the regime could open the door to millions of refugees streaming over the Tumen River border into China and deprive Beijing of a geographical buffer against U.S. forces in the region.

In the last year, however, China has shown signs that it is willing to apply pressure to prevent North Korea's most dangerous behavior.[13] Chinese diplomats have repeatedly called for the resumption of Six Party Talks, its commerce ministry has moved to enforce some of the new sanctions, and Chinese state media have included pointed indications of the party's displeasure with the Kim regime's intransigence.[14] There are other signs as well: in the volatile days of August 2015, Chinese social networking sites showed evidence that China's People's Liberation Army deployed light armored formations to their border with North Korea, and in December, a North Korean pop group abruptly departed Beijing ahead of a prominent scheduled concert.[15]

In this context, North Korea's January 2016 nuclear test could be seen as a public defiance of Chinese President Xi Jinping, just as China had been extending its hand in an attempt to mend poor relations.[16] North Korea's disruptive behavior over the past year underscores the threat that North Korean policies pose to China's national security interests and its standing in the region. It is in this context that President Xi in April 2016 told a group of foreign diplomats that his country "will never allow war or chaos on the peninsula," a warning that seemed to apply to all parties.[17] Further provocations will only strengthen the hand of those in Beijing who support taking a firmer line with Pyongyang.

However, there have also been troubling trends in China-DPRK relations. Beijing's strategy for sanctions and diplomatic contacts evidently intends to maximize its leverage over Pyongyang. U.S. officials should not be surprised if China selectively implements Resolution 2270, modulating the volume of cross-border trade in response to diplomatic developments.[18] Despite the new sanctions, there is little hard evidence that China has placed serious limits on the volume of trade, in part because a great deal of it can pass through loopholes in Resolution 2270 for freight that is "exclusively for livelihood purposes."[19] There are other indications that China continues to look for ways to improve ties. Although North Korean politburo member Ri Su-Yong told Chinese officials that North Korea's policy of expanding its nuclear capabilities is "permanent," his invitation to Beijing to meet with President Xi was probably meant to repair relations.[20] China reportedly continues to allow North Korean hackers to operate from its territory.[21]

China's assessment of its interests in North Korea will critically influence the fate of the Kim Jong-un regime and the efficacy of U.S. policy toward it. U.S. officials cannot depend on China to fully implement Resolution 2270 or to share their views. However, there are indications that factions in China increasingly perceive North Korea as a threat to stability rather than a requirement for it. If so, Beijing may gradually become more willing to discipline Pyongyang for aggressive behavior and its nuclear program. For this reason, encouraging this shift in Beijing's calculus should be a primary objective of U.S. policy toward the region. The United States and its allies should approach this by laying out a sequence of steps, including diplomatic, political, economic, and military, that gradually increase the pressure to resolve the major issues with respect to the Korean Peninsula.

3. *The Task Force finds that South Korea's improving relations with Japan and China present new opportunities for cooperation on North Korea policy.*

In the last year, Japan-ROK relations have made significant steps toward recovery. A November 2015 summit between President Park Geun-hye and Japanese Prime Minister Shinzo Abe succeeded in breaking an almost four-year impasse between the two countries. This brief meeting set the stage for a late December agreement in which Prime Minister Abe apologized to South Korea for Japanese soldiers' forcing Korean women into sexual slavery during World War II, and the Japanese government pledged to fund a foundation administered by the Korean government that would pay reparations to survivors.[22] The historic agreement has now paved the way for broader Japan-ROK coordination on a range of issues, including defense.[23] Although South Korea and Japan, along with the United States, already cooperate on some defense issues—including the 2014 Trilateral Information Sharing Arrangement on North Korea's nuclear and missile threats, which led to a plan to conduct joint missile defense exercises in June 2016— there is ample room to deepen the relationship, which should be done under any future circumstances.[24]

For their part, China and South Korea have jointly committed to urgent steps to limit North Korea's nuclear program.[25] In September 2015, while Kim Jong-un remained ensconced in Pyongyang, President Park attended a military parade in Beijing to commemorate the end of World War II and met with President Xi. In a joint appearance, Park thanked Xi for his country's role in defusing the August crisis; looking forward, both leaders warned the DPRK against new military aggression and called for resumption of the Six Party Talks.[26] Despite concerns over U.S. missile defense assets in South Korea, China and the ROK have maintained frequent and high-level coordination over the North Korean nuclear issue in 2016.[27]

4. *The Task Force finds that South Korea can be an effective representative of shared U.S.-ROK interests, including deterrence signaling to North Korea, coordination with China, and regional diplomacy to promote sanctions enforcement.*

China continues to see the United States as a geostrategic adversary attempting to encircle and isolate it, and North Korea justifies its own vast military as necessary to defend against a U.S. invasion. As a result, U.S. involvement in the region can sometimes provoke strongly negative responses from China and the DPRK. As South Korea improves its relations with Japan and China, it can increasingly play a leadership role in regional deliberations over the North Korean issue. In direct discussions with its northern neighbor, South Korea continues to possess a greater range of policy options than the United States, including the economic, informational, and cultural levers it has used to favorable effect in the recent past. Furthermore, because South Korea is more vulnerable to a North Korean attack, threats that come from Seoul may have greater credibility and be less inflammatory than those from U.S. officials. The alliance's successful management of the August 2015 crisis may prove a useful model: South Korea took the lead on deterrent threats, and the Park administration was able to patiently negotiate a favorable resolution. Last, some potentially valuable forms of regional cooperation will be impossible if they are seen to be imposed by states outside the region; South Korea is well positioned to lead efforts of this kind. Direct U.S.-DPRK negotiations may sometimes be necessary to serve allied interests, but U.S. officials should not automatically assume that they are the best representatives of allied policy.

A DETERIORATING POSITION

5. *Although a negotiated agreement on complete and verifiable denuclearization remains a preferable mechanism for resolving the nuclear issue, the Task Force finds that negotiations are unlikely to eliminate North Korea's nuclear or missile capabilities in the near future. Nonetheless, a new diplomatic approach could potentially freeze North Korea's nuclear and missile programs, establish conditions for increasing pressure if North Korea rejects the proposal, and lay the groundwork for eventual rollback of the regime's nuclear capabilities.*

As North Korea's nuclear capabilities have grown, multilateral negotiations aimed at securing a denuclearized peninsula have ground to a halt. Since the collapse of the 1994 Agreed Framework, international negotiators have focused their attention on the Six Party Talks, a group that includes representatives from China, Japan, North Korea, Russia, South Korea, and the United States. The group's best chance at resuming negotiations on a denuclearization agreement was announced on February 29, 2012, when North Korea agreed to suspend nuclear and missile tests, halt the production of fissile material, and allow International Atomic Energy Agency (IAEA) inspectors back into the country.[28] In exchange, the United States offered security assurances and nutritional assistance that would be delivered to malnourished women and children in North Korea. Just over a month after this Leap Day Agreement, North Korea carried out a failed attempt to launch a satellite into orbit, an effort widely seen as a test of ballistic missile technology. As a result, the agreement collapsed; the United States suspended its aid efforts and wider talks did not take place.[29]

In the years since the failed agreement, the possibility of resuming the Six Party Talks has receded further. North Korean diplomats have reneged on previous willingness to negotiate a denuclearization agreement and have instead begun to insist that the DPRK is a legitimate nuclear power that will not consider restrictions to its nuclear program.[30] In June 2016, North Korea's deputy nuclear envoy reportedly told a forum in Beijing that the Six Party Talks are "dead."[31] North Korean diplomats insist that Washington and Pyongyang should negotiate a peace agreement prior to discussion of the nuclear issue, an approach that U.S. officials have rejected. A peace agreement has been a top priority for the Kim Jong-un regime, which sees it as a way of loosening the country's isolation, improving its security environment, and winning international acceptance of its nuclear, missile, and conventional military capabilities. At the beginning of January 2016, in response to an offer from the North Korean delegation to the United Nations, U.S. diplomats agreed to participate in negotiations that would formally end the Korean War, provided that denuclearization was "part of any such discussion."[32] North Korea rejected this proposal, insisting that the two sides first negotiate a peace treaty. The United States has also repeatedly refused to suspend U.S.-ROK military exercises in return for a DPRK nuclear test freeze.[33]

The United States has offered to discuss resumption of formal negotiations with North Korea at any time, but maintains that comprehensive negotiations can only take place if the regime demonstrates it is willing to work toward complete, verifiable, and irreversible denuclearization (CVID).[34] For its part, China has repeatedly called for the resumption of the Six Party Talks and reportedly increased pressure on its North Korean ally to return to the negotiating table and abandon its nuclear program. However, the United States has rejected China's suggestion to separate peace talks and negotiations on the nuclear issue due to fears that North Korea could stagnate on the latter and seek to progress solely on the former.[35]

Many believe that though denuclearization should remain a primary goal of U.S. policy and the eventual objective of any negotiations, an attempt to condition Six Party Talks on a complete freeze of the program would, in practice, prevent resumption of talks.[36] Moreover, some observers now believe that an exclusive focus on denuclearization impedes negotiations on other measures that could improve stability on the peninsula and contain the spread of nuclear materials and technology.[37] However, it seems clear that recent exchanges over the agenda of multilateral talks have uncovered new issues that could potentially be leveraged to restart them, including the possibility of a freeze on nuclear tests, the scale of U.S.-ROK exercises, and the possibility of an eventual peace agreement.

6. *The Task Force finds that the North Korean state continues to commit grave crimes against humanity, but may be sensitive to international pressure to live up to UN standards on human rights.*

The growing quantity of information now escaping North Korea has revealed the extent of the regime's unconscionable crimes against humanity and the fundamental human rights of its citizens.[38] In March 2013, the UN Human Rights Council established a commission of inquiry (COI) on human rights in North Korea. After interviewing more than three hundred victims, witnesses, and experts, the group reported "systematic, widespread, and gross human rights violations," which "in many instances . . . entailed crimes against humanity."[39] The commission found that North Korea's atrocities include "extermination, murder, enslavement, torture, imprisonment, rape, forced abortions and other sexual violence, persecution on political, religious, racial and gender grounds, the forcible transfer of populations, the enforced disappearance of persons and the inhumane act of knowingly causing prolonged starvation."[40] It found that citizens are also subject to an "almost complete denial of the right to freedom of thought, conscience, and religion"; deprivation of information; constant surveillance; economic and gender discrimination; and deliberate geographic segregation for the purposes of control, among other abuses.[41] Using overhead imagery, the commission estimated that "between 80,000 and 120,000 [people] are currently detained in four large political prison camps."[42]

Despite these violations, the DPRK inexplicably remains a member of the United Nations and is party to four international human rights treaties, as well as the Genocide Convention and the Geneva Conventions.[43] In this regard, North Korea has enjoyed the protection of Russia and China, which often deny the authority of international legal bodies to investigate, sanction, and prosecute crimes against humanity. South Korea and others have questioned why the regime is allowed to retain its status as a member of the United Nations.[44]

Surprisingly, after years of ignoring UN resolutions and reports, North Korea actively engaged with UN bodies following the issuance of the COI findings. North Korean diplomats worked to have provisions on crimes against humanity and accountability excised from General Assembly resolutions. When this failed, North Korea again turned away. In advance of a Human Rights Council meeting in September 2015, a foreign ministry spokesman claimed that the meeting was a "political maneuver aimed at overthrowing our regime," claiming that the "evidence is nothing more than lies from North Korean defectors."[45] In the same period, North Korea extended an invitation to the UN High Commissioner for Human Rights, but then failed to make the visit possible.[46] The foreign minister later announced that North Korea would not cooperate with the council. This newfound sensitivity may be tied to repeated attempts by the Kim Jong-un regime to convince other nations to improve economic and political relations with his country and to treat it as a responsible member of the international community.[47]

> 7. *The Task Force finds that the recent expansion of the sanctions regime is a necessary step in exerting pressure on North Korea. However, expanded and sustained efforts are required to ensure that they are rigorously implemented and have the desired effects, including measures to provide amenable states with material assistance and to pressure those that illegally trade with or finance North Korea.*

North Korea continues to resist a range of international sanctions over its nuclear and missile programs. Previous UN Security Council resolutions prohibited member states from buying or selling heavy weapons, including armored vehicles and aircraft, as well as conducting financial transactions that could assist North Korea in developing nuclear weapons and ballistic missiles. Under these resolutions, member states are required to inspect and seize cargo entering the DPRK if it may relate to prohibited military activities.[48] The sanctions regime, which developed over the course of a decade in response to repeated North Korean violations, is calibrated to restrain North Korea's military advancement by denying it access to foreign technology and financing necessary to undertake research, development, and procurement of advanced systems. The sanctions have largely succeeded in shrinking North Korea's customer base for conventional arms export, yet they have failed to shift the regime's calculus on its nuclear and missile programs, which continue to develop through mostly indigenous resources.

Since 2006, North Korea has developed an extensive clandestine network of diplomats and foreign nationals to circumvent the sanctions regime.[49] There are indications that a range of countries and terrorist organizations continue to deal with North Korea for aircraft maintenance (Ethiopia), ammunition (Tanzania), personnel training (Uganda), rockets (Hamas and Hezbollah via Iran), and others.[50] In addition, there is evidence that North Korea has recently cooperated with Iran and Syria in the development and transfer of a wide variety of ballistic missiles, as well as nuclear technology.[51]

Immediately following North Korea's nuclear test in January 2016, the U.S. government moved to tighten unilateral sanctions on North Korea. The extensive sanctions that helped keep Iran at the negotiation table and resulted in the 2015 Joint Comprehensive Plan of Action convinced many that U.S. sanctions toward North Korea were comparatively lenient.[52] In response, the president issued a new Executive Order that markedly expanded the government's authority to designate North Korean officials for sanctions.[53] Soon after, the U.S. Congress overwhelmingly passed HR 757, the North Korea Sanctions and Policy Enhancement Act of 2016, which imposes mandatory sanctions on individuals and entities who aid North Korea in a variety of illicit activities, including trade in "significant arms or related materiel," censorship, money laundering, cyberattacks, and—for the first time—human rights abuses.[54] On June 1, 2016, the U.S. Department of the Treasury designated North Korea as a primary money laundering concern under Section 311 of the USA Patriot Act, further restricting the regime's access to the international financial system.[55]

On March 2, 2016, two months after North Korea conducted its fourth nuclear test, the UN Security Council unanimously voted to adopt Resolution 2270, which is a significant expansion of the international sanctions regime. The resolution expands the current prohibition on arms trade to cover all items that would enable North Korea to improve its conventional forces and extends lists of proliferation-sensitive items, individuals and entities subject to asset freezes and travel bans, and prohibited luxury goods sought by the regime's elite. Furthermore, the resolution imposes several new measures, including legally obligating UN member states to "inspect the cargo within or transiting through their territory, including their airports, seaports, and free trade zones, that has originated in the DPRK, or that is destined for the DPRK."[56] Additionally, member states are prohibited from importing North Korean coal, iron, gold, rare earth minerals, and other metals if the proceeds might benefit the regime's nuclear or missile programs. The resolution also includes major new restrictions on diplomats, trade assistance, and financial services suspected of aiding North Korean weapons programs.[57]

Resolution 2270 is an encouraging step, but its potential to affect the North Korean regime's behavior is contingent on strict implementation of the new requirements. Cargo inspections are a significant barrier not only to nuclear proliferation and illicit arms sales, but also to North Korea's few remaining legitimate exports. This step, combined with financial and export restrictions, could make an appreciable dent in North Korea's economy, impeding the regime's ability to fund nuclear and missile development and continue operating its conventional armed forces. However, these measures require significant attention and funding to implement fully. They will tax the navies, ports, intelligence services, diplomatic corps, and political will of a large group of states, including critical transit hubs in Southeast Asia.

8. *The Task Force finds that North Korea's development of the capability to deliver a nuclear warhead on a long-range ballistic missile would dramatically increase its ability to threaten the United States and its allies.*

After North Korea abandoned the February 2012 Leap Day Agreement, the Obama administration adopted a policy of "strategic patience" toward the DPRK.[58] This policy has meant strengthening the U.S.-ROK alliance against a range of military aggression while affirming a willingness to resume negotiations with North Korea.

Yet North Korea's nuclear program continues to advance steadily.[59] In January 2016, North Korea claimed to have tested a hydrogen bomb, though experts believe it was more likely a boosted fission device, a type of weapon that increases yield by including some fusion fuel in a normal fission explosive package. Two months later, the regime claimed to have successfully developed a miniaturized nuclear warhead that could be fitted to a ballistic missile.[60] It then threatened to test this warhead along with a vehicle that would allow the warhead to survive reentry into the earth's atmosphere.[61] Should this occur, the test would cause North Korea to edge dangerously close to the critical threshold in which it could credibly threaten to deliver a nuclear weapon on a ballistic missile.[62] However, the regime has yet to test a ballistic missile that would be an effective delivery system (presumed to be the KN-08 missile) or a reentry vehicle.[63] The volatile spring also saw two test fires of a new submarine-launched ballistic missile, a new engine configuration for an ICBM, a test of a new multiple launch rocket artillery system (MLRS), a satellite launch, and five failed tests of the Musudan intermediate-range missile, as well as one partial success in June 2016 (figure 3).[64]

Based on publicly available information about North Korean fissile material production, estimates suggest that North Korea could have

FIGURE 3: NORTH KOREAN NUCLEAR AND MISSILE TESTS (1998–2016*)

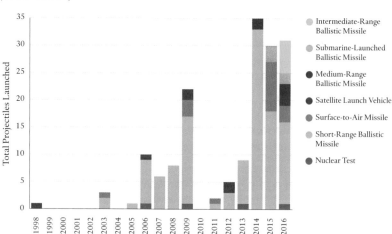

*Current as of July 20, 2016

between thirteen and twenty-one nuclear weapons as of June 2016 and still more fissile material under pessimistic assumptions about the program.[65] The five-megawatt electric (MW$_e$) reactor at Yongbyon, which was shut down in the mid-2000s during Six Party Talks, has resumed operation since 2013.[66] In June, observers in Seoul and Washington detected signs that North Korea had begun another round of plutonium reprocessing, increasing its stock available for warhead production and expanding the DPRK arsenal by an estimated four to six weapons since the beginning of 2015.[67] Meanwhile, unclassified estimates assume that the North Korean uranium enrichment program continues to develop, though sources are uncertain about the existence or location of a second enrichment facility beyond the centrifuge plant at Yongbyon, which widens the confidence bounds of fissile material estimates.[68] Alarmingly, North Korea has demonstrated a willingness to proliferate nuclear equipment, expertise, and fissile material when it assisted with construction of the Deir ez-Zor reactor in Syria.[69] These advancements in its nuclear and missile capabilities have brought North Korea to a critical moment for U.S. defense planning.

9. *The Task Force finds that although U.S.-ROK deterrence policy may have succeeded in preventing major military attacks since 2010, the frequency and severity of North Korea's aggressive behavior will likely increase as its nuclear and sub-conventional capabilities continue to develop.*

As its nuclear weapons and missile programs continue to advance, North Korea's leadership may believe that it has new options to coerce and aggress against the U.S.-ROK alliance.[70] For example, Pyongyang may presume that it can employ a nuclear weapon in a limited way to force the U.S.-ROK alliance to back down from a militarized dispute or a limited armed conflict.[71] If the DPRK leadership thinks that it can prevail at the nuclear level, it may also believe that the alliance will lack resolve to respond decisively to military provocations at the sub-conventional level, including limited attacks with indirect fire, or special forces, maritime, or cyber operations like the November 2014 attack against Sony. This, in turn, may lead the regime to attempt to blackmail the United States and South Korea into conceding militarized disputes on favorable terms.[72] In some cases, such as the Sony hack, the United States has lacked a coherent and resolute response, but new legal authority can enable U.S. agencies to work with allies in developing a ready plan of action for future intrusions.[73]

Although North Korea's vast conventional forces remain a grave threat to South Korea, the quality and readiness of these forces have declined in recent years as the regime invests larger portions of its limited available funding into its nuclear program.[74] The Pentagon assesses that the DPRK's Korean People's Army "retains the capability to inflict serious damage on the ROK, despite significant resource shortfalls and aging hardware."[75] Imports of heavy weapons, including mechanized and armored vehicles, fixed- and rotary-wing aircraft, and modern ships have halted as a result of UN sanctions and funding constraints. To compensate, the regime has made significant investments in conventional short-range surface-to-surface missiles, cyber capabilities, and its sizable Special Operations forces (SOF). North Korea's new MLRS system, which Pyongyang has reportedly deployed widely along the demilitarized zone (DMZ), increases its ability to threaten Seoul with artillery fires.[76]

These developments suggest that North Korea has developed an increasingly sophisticated but risky operational concept, in which it may attempt to carry out limited attacks in multiple sub-conventional domains and potentially deter an allied response by threatening civilians in Japan and South Korea with nuclear and conventional attacks. If so, Pyongyang may feel increasingly empowered to launch more frequent and more damaging provocations and to escalate the resulting crisis.

10. *The Task Force finds that current trends, if allowed to continue, will predictably, progressively, and gravely threaten U.S. national interests and those of its allies.*

With each passing year, North Korea develops its nuclear and missile programs, continues to perpetrate its crimes against humanity, and steadily destabilizes a region critical to U.S. national interests.[77] As North Korea advances its nuclear capabilities, each successive crisis has greater potential for catastrophe. The regime in Pyongyang is developing the capability to order a nuclear strike on an American city, forcing a future U.S. president into an even more difficult position. North Korea's ability to evade sanctions increases by the year; Resolution 2270's expanded legal authority will do little to help if new sanctions are not strictly enforced and adapted in future years.[78] In short, the options available to the United States are narrowing and North Korea's are expanding. Reversing these trends will require an urgent shift in U.S. policy.

Recommendations

A SHARPER CHOICE

The Task Force's finding that current trends will predictably, progressively, and gravely threaten U.S. national interests requires a change in U.S. policy toward North Korea. The strengthened sanctions passed in early 2016 represent a significant shift in policy toward North Korea, but will not be sufficient to compel the North Korean regime to abandon its nuclear and missile programs, observe a stabilizing military posture, and respect the human rights of its citizens. Barring a major change on the peninsula, achieving these goals will require a broad negotiated agreement. Cognizant that this agreement may not come soon, the United States and its allies should prepare to deter and defend against a hostile North Korea, including by expanding U.S.-ROK-Japan cooperation on enhanced deterrent measures and actively enforcing strict sanctions against North Korea.

To get North Korea back to the bargaining table, the United States should commit itself to a sequence of steps that not only imposes escalating costs on continued defiance, but also provides incentives for cooperation. This sequence should be calibrated to credibly signal to North Korea that the United States and its allies will continually increase pressure until substantive talks resume on acceptable terms. Collectively, these measures will sharpen North Korea's choice, outlining clear expectations and consequences that will result from defiance. Careful sequencing maximizes opportunities to coordinate with China and is important both to present opportunity and to demonstrate that delay will become increasingly costly.

As an initial step, U.S. officials should propose restructured negotiations that provide genuine incentives for Pyongyang to negotiate on a series of expanding issues, culminating in complete and verifiable denuclearization and a treaty that will end the Korean War. If Pyongyang refuses to comply with this proposal, the United States should authorize new military measures to deny North Korea the benefits of its actions and to strengthen deterrence of military attacks, as well as to impose new sanctions that more severely restrict the regime's funding sources. Escalating costs will not be easy; the United States and its allies will likely pay a price for some of these measures, including possible violent retribution from Pyongyang. Because it is not the policy of the U.S. government to induce a collapse of the North Korean regime, these policies will have to be calibrated carefully.

China's policy toward North Korea will critically affect this effort and the fate of Northeast Asia. A transformed China policy toward North Korea should be the central objective of U.S. policy toward maritime Asia and of the U.S.-China relationship, which will shape the region well into the twenty-first century. North Korea's continued development of nuclear weapons and destabilizing military actions will suppress efforts to improve this relationship and prevent the emergence of a stable and prosperous regional order. For these reasons, improved U.S.-China relations require progress on the North Korean issue.

To convince China of its shared interest with the United States in finding a comprehensive and lasting resolution to the North Korean problem, U.S. officials should approach China with a new proposal that outlines a sharper choice: work with the United States and its allies to realize a stable, just, and nuclear-free Korean Peninsula, or the United States and its allies will be forced to take additional steps to achieve these results over time. This should be done through carefully sequenced and calibrated steps designed to gradually but discernibly increase the pressure toward successful resolution of the peace treaty, denuclearization, and peaceful and gradual reunification of the Korean Peninsula. Although Beijing is not likely to pressure Pyongyang over human rights, China can help get North Korea back to the negotiating table by withdrawing material support, enforcing sanctions, and applying diplomatic pressure. For example, Beijing could act to curtail the trade of energy resources and consumer goods from maritime shipping and across the Tumen River, clamp down on criminal activity in China that raises revenue for the regime, prevent North Korea's cyber division from using Chinese networks and territory to launch attacks around the world, and signal continued willingness to cooperate with the United States on North Korean issues at the United Nations.

To encourage China to participate and assuage its concern that a moderate North Korea would hasten China's encirclement by U.S. forces, the United States should offer a new dialogue on the future of the peninsula that includes discussions about the future disposition of U.S. forces. This dialogue should attempt to coordinate planning in the event of a collapse, crisis, or major attack and convey that it is not U.S. policy to cause a collapse of the DPRK regime. As part of these talks, U.S. officials can also assure China that its coercive diplomatic, economic, and military policies are exceptional responses to the unique, rapid, and explosive threat posed by North Korea.

Simultaneously, the United States should support President Park's call for five-party talks. This format—consisting of China, Japan, Russia, South Korea, and the United States—allows the parties to share information about North Korea, to plan negotiating strategy for the next round of multilateral talks, and to discuss the future security order of Northeast Asia.

However, for practical and unavoidable reasons, major improvement of the U.S.-China relationship will prove impossible without progress on North Korea. U.S. officials should demonstrate to China that North Korea's failure to respond to this new approach will require the United States to invest more heavily in the region—tighten its alliances, enhance its military presence, and sanction entities that assist North Korea—all steps that will strain the U.S.-China relationship.

To ensure that U.S. policy on North Korea supports broader national interests, each component of this policy—long-range planning, negotiations strategy, support for human rights, sanctions, and deterrence and defense—needs to remain consistent with a vision for a stable and prosperous Northeast Asia that U.S. allies have a role in leading. If North Korea policy becomes detached from regional policy, both are likely to fail.

PROMOTE A STABLE AND PROSPEROUS NORTHEAST ASIA

I. *The Task Force recommends that the United States and its allies engage China as soon as possible to plan for the future of the Korean Peninsula. These talks, both trilateral and in a five-party format, should plan for militarized crises, collapse scenarios, and the role of a unified Korea in Northeast Asian security.*

To ensure that its North Korea strategy is consistent with a vision for a stable and peaceful Northeast Asia, the United States should engage regional states in joint planning for a stable Asia.[79]

Collapse of the Six Party process has also meant the loss of an important consultative mechanism for regional stability. To recover some of these functions and establish a venue to coordinate the resumption of multilateral negotiations to denuclearize the peninsula, President Park in January 2016 suggested convening the five parties that negotiate with North Korea. Five-party talks on this model could help the parties share their assessments of Pyongyang's likely negotiating strategy and perhaps draw up a proposal to convince North Korea to return to talks.[80] Moreover, the talks could allow the parties to share information on and coordinate their responses to the possibility of an infectious pandemic in North Korea, a nuclear accident, a humanitarian crisis, and other scenarios that could yield instability and conflict on the peninsula.[81] They might also agree to coordinate in preventing the spread of nuclear weapons to new states, which is critical to the long-term stability of Northeast Asia because proliferation would raise the risk of conflict both with the nuclear aspirant and with North Korea. In this way, the parties might decrease the likelihood that operations on and around the peninsula could result in miscalculation or contact between their forces.

Although the likelihood of a collapse of the North Korean regime has decreased in recent years, it remains a possibility under several scenarios and would have large and unintended consequences for North Korea's neighbors. A vast outflow of impoverished North Korean refugees; unsecured nuclear, chemical, and biological material along with substantial caches of conventional weaponry; and the potential need to conduct operations against a large, armed insurgency in difficult terrain are just some of the potential challenges of a collapse scenario. U.S. officials report that China has repeatedly declined to discuss its planning for these scenarios with them, raising the likelihood that U.S. and Chinese forces could find themselves working at cross-purposes at a time of elevated tensions with their forces in close proximity. The Task Force recommends that U.S. policymakers continue working with China on this issue at each stage of U.S. policy and conduct detailed planning on possible collapse scenarios in the context of the U.S.-ROK-Japan alliance.[82]

The United States and South Korea can seek to break the impasse with China over long-range planning by embedding collapse planning in a broader dialogue about the future of the Korean Peninsula. Together, the allies should develop a set of reassurances that unification will not damage China's interests. For example, South Korea can work to assure China that its economic interests in North Korea will be respected during unification. It can guarantee that Chinese investments will either remain in place or be compensated by the central government. Further dialogues can de-conflict plans for border control, management of refugees, port access, and other issues of concern. Combined Forces Command officials can develop briefings about their plans for operations on the peninsula to encourage Chinese officials in the People's Liberation Army to share their own planning. De-conflicting U.S.-ROK-China military planning is critical to avoiding a wider conflict in the event that UN forces have to operate in and around North Korea and therefore to the vital national security interests of all three countries.

The United States has and will maintain a steadfast commitment to ensure that South Korea remains free and secure. For the foreseeable future, a sizable U.S. presence on the peninsula is necessary to defend South Korea against the threat from its northern neighbor, and the United States will not abrogate its alliance commitment in any event. However, the United States and South Korea should jointly develop and present to China conditions under which the alliance would consider revising the number and disposition of U.S. forces on the peninsula. They should make clear that force levels are and will be calibrated to the severity of the threat from North Korea; if and when the threat abates due to reform or replacement of the DPRK regime, the alliance will consider a commensurate adjustment to U.S. force posture on the peninsula. U.S. military presence on the peninsula is a guarantee of the safety, freedom, and prosperity of South Korea and is not intended to encircle or contain China. The imperative to defend against North Korea does not entail an inherent interest in sustaining a certain force level on the peninsula permanently. In any event, the U.S.-ROK military alliance should remain and retain the right to deploy U.S. forces as circumstances require.

This proposal aims to alleviate one of the primary obstacles to the resolution of the North Korean problem. Beijing worries that the fall of Pyongyang would lead to a unified peninsula under U.S. control, deepening China's encirclement and bringing the most powerful military in the world to its border. However, if U.S. forces on the peninsula are indexed to the threat level, it may encourage China to see North Korea as more of an impediment to its long-term national security interests and less of a necessary buffer against U.S. hegemony. This could incentivize China to restrict North Korea's ability to threaten its neighbors. In this way, U.S.-ROK policy would encourage China to take a more assertive role, rather than, from its perspective, punish it for doing so. Although the United States will likely remain the guarantor of South Korean security far into the twenty-first century, initiating this discussion may help promote a stable Northeast Asia over the long run and redound to the benefit of South Korea and Japan, as well as China.

The importance of South Korea and Japan in a stable and prosperous Northeast Asia cannot be overstated. Developments in North Korea critically affect the security of both countries and their standing in the region. For this reason, U.S. policy on North Korea needs to promote a regional order in which both states play a leading role in safeguarding the rule of law, human rights, and strategic stability in a region critical to U.S. interests. By jointly conducting military operations to deter North Korea, planning for major scenarios on the peninsula, and engaging in coordinated diplomacy with China on the North Korea issue, the United States, South Korea, and Japan can promote a brighter future for the region than they could in isolation.

RESTRUCTURE NEGOTIATIONS

II. *The Task Force recommends that the United States move quickly to propose restructured negotiations to limit North Korea's nuclear and missile programs and work toward denuclearization and a comprehensive peace agreement.*

Although a negotiated agreement to free the peninsula of nuclear weapons will remain the primary objective of U.S. policy, the Task Force finds that this goal has become improbable in the near future. Both to pursue this goal and to promote national security interests, the Task Force recommends that the United States propose restructuring negotiations with North Korea on the expectation that intermediate agreements on other issues can demonstrate the benefits of cooperation and establish an incentive to achieve a wider agreement further down the line.

The first step in this model will be to find agreement on the enabling conditions for talks. The next administration should review U.S. policy on negotiations and communicate clear preconditions for the resumption of formal multilateral negotiations. It should formally dispel the mistaken perception that it places preconditions on informal talks with

North Korea and that it demands unilateral steps prior to the start of formal negotiations. Instead, the United States should insist on three conditions for resumption of talks. First, all parties should agree to reaffirm the principles of the Joint Statement of 2005, including its commitment to a nonnuclear peninsula and a stable and lawful regional order.[83] Second, negotiations need to make consistent progress on the nuclear issue at each stage in the negotiations to ensure that North Korea cannot benefit by stalling on denuclearization. Third, because it will be impossible to negotiate while the DPRK carries out nuclear and long-range missile tests, the United States should insist on a moratorium on all tests of nuclear explosives and missiles with a range-payload capability greater than existing Scud missiles, whether declared to be ballistic missiles or civil space launch vehicles. Because North Korea still has not tested a long-range ballistic missile with a reentry vehicle, a test moratorium will constitute a meaningful restraint on the program while negotiators seek a verified freeze on its other aspects. In exchange and if requested by Pyongyang, the U.S. and South Korean governments may, for as long as negotiations are progressing, consent to supply nutritional assistance to the North Korean civilian population, provided that NGOs can certify that these supplies are not being diverted to the military; U.S. and South Korean officials may also consider modifications to the scale and content of U.S.-ROK joint military exercises.

Initial negotiations should focus on attaining a verified freeze in North Korea's nuclear capabilities. A complete verified freeze of the nuclear program would require six restrictions: no nuclear tests; no missile launches, whether declared to be ballistic missiles or civil space launch vehicles with a range-payload capability greater than the DPRK's existing Scud missiles; no plutonium reprocessing; no uranium enrichment; suspension of reactor operations at Yongbyon; and readmission of the IAEA to North Korea to monitor the nuclear elements of the freeze, both at declared facilities and with the approval of the five parties (China, Japan, Russia, South Korea, United States). Additionally, the parties can explore conventional arms control measures; limitations on missile development; steps to prevent the spread of nuclear weapons, technology, and materials beyond North Korea's borders; early access for IAEA inspectors to specific North Korean nuclear facilities that Pyongyang has declared to be for civilian purposes; and measures to promote the welfare of North Korea's citizens, starting with allowing the International Committee of the Red Cross to access political prison camps. In the initial phase, U.S., South Korean, and North Korean negotiators can also begin to discuss the terms of a peace treaty that will end the Korean War.

The eventual objective of these staged negotiations is to achieve North Korea's complete denuclearization and reentry into the Nuclear Nonproliferation Treaty. In exchange, the regional powers would commit to sign a comprehensive peace treaty, normalize relations, lift the appropriate sanctions, and allow North Korea's integration into the global financial system. Full normalization of relations and sanctions relief will require major progress on North Korea's human rights position, including the release of all political prisoners and their families, a full accounting and voluntary repatriation of all persons abducted from foreign countries, nondiscriminatory food aid distribution monitored by aid workers who are guaranteed full nationwide access, freedom to leave the country and return without punishment, and ending the information blockade imposed on North Korea's citizens by the government.[84]

The main negotiations can take place under the Six Party Talks format, but certain issues can be resolved in smaller talks among North and South Korea, the United States, and China. This format, in which Korean representatives could be the primary negotiators, can be used to negotiate preconditions prior to the start of talks as well as the terms of an armistice that will be signed at the end of the process. Limiting the membership of the negotiations on difficult issues may encourage China to apply pressure on North Korea. The Task Force recommends that U.S. negotiators remain open to other formats for talks that could potentially be productive.

PROTECT HUMAN RIGHTS

III. *The Task Force recommends that the United States work with allies, NGOs, and the United Nations system to escalate pressure on North Korea to respect the human rights of its citizens.*

Support for human rights is an integral component of U.S. foreign policy, which holds that human rights must be inviolate and that support for them is neither a bargaining chip nor a weapon. The United States should not consent to normalize relations so long as North Korea continues to perpetrate crimes against humanity. Exceptional steps are necessary to reverse North Korea's egregious, consistent, and willful noncompliance with UN human rights resolutions and preserve the integrity of the United Nations.

To this end, the Task Force recommends that as part of the initial announcement of the new strategy, the United States should work with its allies and partners to jointly signal their intention to execute a campaign of continually escalating pressure on North Korea on human rights issues as long as the DPRK remains noncompliant with UN human rights resolutions.[85] They should make it known that the DPRK's continued defiance of UN human rights resolutions puts into question the regime's standing in that organization. In addition to designating North Korean officials for sanctions under U.S. law, the United States should work with its allies to present North Korea with a choice: make rapid improvements to its human rights record or these countries will support suspension of North Korea's credentials at the United Nations.

Suspension of a state's credentials is not the same as expulsion from the organization: without credentials, a state may officially retain its membership, but it is prohibited from attending or participating in UN General Assembly proceedings. There is precedent for this step. In 1974, the General Assembly passed Resolution 3206, which endorsed the recommendation of the Credentials Committee to suspend South Africa's participation over its continued disregard for Security Council resolutions condemning apartheid.[86] The General Assembly also called on the Security Council to consider full expulsion of South Africa from the organization, but the measure was vetoed by France, the United Kingdom, and the United States.[87] South Africa retained this status until 1994, when the country's credentials were restored following its transition to democracy.[88]

In the last two years, the commission of inquiry and increasing information from within the regime have helped raise international awareness about North Korean crimes against humanity. In 2014 and again in 2015, the General Assembly recommended that the Security Council refer the case of North Korea to the International Criminal Court for prosecution of crimes against humanity, which diplomats expect would be blocked by Russia and China.[89] This flood of international concern may permit action in the United Nations. As a first step, the United States should work with its global allies to signal to North Korea that they will support suspension of its credentials without rapid progress on human rights. To prevent this suspension, North Korea will be required to, within two years, receive a visit from the UN High Commissioner for Human Rights and a mission from the UN Special Rapporteur on Human Rights in the DPRK, and show substantial progress in implementing its human rights obligations under UN treaties. These steps may be agreed through the UN system or as part of multilateral negotiations with China, South Korea, and the United States.

Each year, when the UN Credentials Committee meets at the start of each General Assembly session, it can consult with UN human rights officials to determine whether North Korea has met the above conditions and should have its credentials reinstated.

Second, the United States should support enhanced information operations carried out by South Korea and nongovernmental organizations, which aim to inform North Korea's population about the outside world and, in so doing, could lay the groundwork for voluntary evolution of the state. To do this, the U.S. Congress should appropriate funding to support expanded Voice of America programming and NGOs that are working to penetrate an increasingly porous censorship regime. Priorities for funding include increased power for medium-wave radio transmissions, more radio broadcasts, and cultivation of North Korean defectors to serve as journalists for these stations. These broadcasts should not focus on antigovernment political propaganda, but rather should consist mainly of business and economic information, agricultural instruction, weather forecasts, and information about daily life outside of North Korea, including housing, food, and medicines, as well as Korean pop music, talk radio, and gossip.

In addition, support should be provided to NGOs that require additional funding for their efforts to deliver information to North Koreans on USB drives. These USB drives can contain diverse sources from agriculture and economics textbooks to novels and literature that convey a portrait of everyday life free from the Kim regime. Over time, these efforts could gradually undermine the regime's monopoly on information, strengthen emerging market forces, and cultivate the foundation for a different system of government for the people of North Korea in the future.

Last, the United States should materially support and join efforts to gather information about the regime's human rights violations to prepare for the day when its worst offenders are brought to justice. In recent years, this issue has received increased attention.[90] In 2015, the United Nations opened an office in Seoul to document human rights abuses "with a view to accountability."[91] South Korea's new human rights act provides for the establishment of a documentation center, which will compile testimony and data in addition to that already uncovered by the COI and various NGOs.[92] In March 2016, the UN Human Rights

Council established a panel of experts "to focus on issues of accountability."[93] These efforts to prepare for accountability, including by continuing to apply sanctions to North Korean officials who perpetrate human rights abuses, could have a powerful deterrent effect today and may also help undermine the regime's internal legitimacy. The United States should provide information to these organizations, along with material, technical, and rhetorical support when possible.

ENFORCE SANCTIONS AND ESCALATE FINANCIAL PRESSURE

IV. *The Task Force recommends that the United States invest in rigorous enforcement of the sanctions regime and apply escalating pressure on North Korea's illicit activities.*

Severe economic pressure on the North Korean regime is a necessary way to compel compliance with its nuclear, military, and human rights obligations to the United Nations and a central instrument of U.S. and international coercive power. However, sanctions alone are unlikely to be enough. The Task Force recommends that the next administration work with allies, countries in the region, and the U.S. Congress to mount a more assertive and consistent campaign to sanction the full range of North Korea's illicit behavior. The sanctions authority granted by Resolution 2270 is a good start, but the resolution's effective impact will depend on the extent to which the sanctions are enforced by states in the region. Strictly enforcing Resolution 2270, including the mandate to inspect all cargo entering or exiting North Korea, can not only apply economic pressure to the regime, but also help limit corruption and criminal activity that emanates from the regime and prevent the spread of nuclear material and technology. New provocations should prompt the Security Council to close loopholes in Resolution 2270, especially the unenforceable provision that allows trade for the "livelihood purposes" but not for military purposes.[94] Implementation of multilateral sanctions should be accompanied by new rounds of U.S. financial sanctions to apply escalating pressure to the regime's source of funding.

To ensure that regional states have the resources necessary to enforce the new sanctions, the United States should act quickly to assist its partners in setting up a standing multilateral mechanism to coordinate implementation of UN sanctions, including inspection of North Korean cargo and, if necessary, interdiction at sea of ships suspected of transporting it, beginning with the most suspect shipments. This group should be specifically dedicated to the enforcement of the DPRK sanctions and would ideally include all states in the region, including China. For this mechanism to succeed, it must be perceived as a regional initiative, not as an extension of UN or U.S. authority. For this reason, interested outside parties like the United States and the European Union could provide assistance to the effort in an advisory capacity. China should be encouraged to take a prominent and constructive role in this process, commensurate with its claims to regional responsibility. If it demurs, the participating states can coordinate sanctions enforcement and maritime interdiction on their own, including, if necessary, in the Yellow Sea. Enforcement of the shipping restrictions may require the United States to expand its naval capacity assigned to the mission and the region.

The process can serve as a clearinghouse for resources necessary for sanctions enforcement, including shipping information and intelligence, as well as financial, material, legal, technical, and military assistance to states that request it.[95] This process could also promote strict sanctions enforcement by serving as a mechanism to discipline reticent or distracted countries that might otherwise allow implementation to slip.[96] The new organization should seek to reform openly noncompliant states, such as Vietnam and Myanmar; motivate states with mixed records, such as Thailand, Cambodia, Malaysia, Hong Kong, and Taiwan; and reinforce states such as Singapore and the Philippines that are actively working to meet their obligations. This new mechanism will build on the experience of existing multilateral instruments such as the Proliferation Security Initiative to specifically enforce the multifaceted UN Security Council sanctions on North Korea.[97]

To ensure that the United States and its allies can continue to escalate economic pressure on the regime, they should initiate a consistent campaign to sanction and restrict the full range of North Korea's criminal activities. Financial crimes, money laundering, corruption, human rights abuses, and malicious cyber activity have all received too little attention from the international community and should be subject to strict sanctions, financial pressure, and law enforcement. Efforts to use financial measures such as Section 311 of the Patriot Act, as against Banco Delta Asia in 2005, have been important but inconsistent. The U.S. Treasury's recent designation of North Korea as a "primary money laundering concern" under Section 311 is a good starting point, as is its June 2016 designation of senior North Korean officials for human rights abuses, including Kim Jong-un.[98] As long as North Korea continues to refuse negotiations or conduct destabilizing provocations, the United States should continue to designate new individuals and entities for criminal activity as new information becomes available. The U.S. government should also work with foreign partners to levy parallel sanctions against these entities; a consistent and expanding multilateral sanctions regime would be a powerful complement to efforts to improve North Korea's human rights and criminal practices through the United Nations.[99] In the United States, the next steps should be to establish private rights of action so that private companies can bring legal suits against the countries and companies doing business with North Korea, and to work with China to identify, designate, and sanction entities that conduct corrupt and criminal activities under Chinese and international law.[100]

This is an area where the interests of the United States, its allies, and China substantially overlap. North Korea is a source of corruption and criminal activity for the entire region. In May 2016, reports emerged of North Korean cyberattacks on Asian banks that made off with more than $100 million.[101] All states have an interest in restricting this kind of illegal activity within their borders. The exchange of information through a regional sanctions enforcement mechanism should provide tools for law enforcement to crack down on Pyongyang's criminal exports.

Last, the United States should signal to other governments that it will actively designate and sanction foreign companies and individuals that facilitate North Korea's illegal activities, which foster crime and corruption across the region.

STRENGTHEN DETERRENCE AND DEFENSE

V. *The Task Force recommends that the United States, South Korea, and Japan move expeditiously to tighten collaboration and strengthen their deterrence and defense posture.*

Currently, the United States maintains strong alliances with both Japan and South Korea. The Obama administration has pressed both allies to participate in closer trilateral cooperation, which in 2010 led to a trilateral statement that "the DPRK's provocative and belligerent behavior threatens all three countries and will be met with solidarity from all three countries."[102] In light of North Korea's increasing capability to threaten the three partners in diverse ways, the attendant benefits of coordination, and improved Japan-ROK relations, the Task Force recommends expanding this declaration.

Specifically, the United States, South Korea, and Japan should issue a collective security commitment declaring that a North Korean attack against any one of these states is an attack against all.[103] The three countries should aspire to formalize this relationship as a trilateral alliance vis-à-vis North Korea as fast as political conditions allow. Both steps will help facilitate cooperation on issues of joint concern and make it clear that North Korea cannot hope to prevent a collective reaction to attacks.[104] For example, strategists have long worried that Pyongyang may attempt to cover a limited attack by striking U.S. forces on Okinawa. This strike could create tensions between South Korea and Japan that would inhibit a unified response and allow the regime to deescalate the crisis. A resolute collective security declaration would disabuse Pyongyang of this notion. The three partners should immediately expand their defense cooperation to explore an expanded intelligence-sharing arrangement, joint maritime operations (including antisubmarine operations and counter-SOF missions), and regular joint exercises. The three partners should also coordinate to build capacity of naval operations to interdict and inspect North Korean cargo and then to implement the mandate. In addition, they should pursue a regional joint missile defense architecture to improve tracking and interception of North Korean missiles (though it need not be integrated with the entire U.S. National Missile Defense system). The collective security declaration should also extend to a cyberattack against critical infrastructure in all three countries, as the North Atlantic Treaty Organization (NATO) has done.[105] Including this provision in the collective security agreement would help the countries jointly assess threats and provide for a commonality of doctrine for cyber operations, thereby increasing the capability and credibility of a joint response. In issuing their declaration, leaders of the three countries should be clear that the declaration and increased trilateral cooperation is specifically directed at the North Korean threat.

Coincident with their collective security declaration, the three partners should clarify and declare their deterrent posture toward North Korea. To deter Pyongyang from initiating dangerous new provocation cycles, U.S., South Korean, and Japanese officials should jointly signal that future aggression will be met with an active and proportionate response, which may include strikes against military targets inside

North Korea. Although the U.S.-ROK alliance has never ruled out this option, it has also never carried out such an operation. Halting the cycle of provocation will require holding at risk North Korean units and positions that believe they can strike at South Korean territory with impunity. The joint statement should also reiterate that the DPRK has not attained and will never be permitted to attain a condition of mutual assured destruction with the three partners. Allied officials should declare that although they do not intend to topple the North Korean regime, widespread civilian casualties from invasion, indirect fire, or the use of nuclear weapons could make this unavoidable.

While trilateral cooperation is under way, the United States and South Korea should continue to strengthen their deterrence posture toward North Korea to dissuade it from even more destabilizing behavior in three ways.

First, although the United States will continue to extend nuclear deterrence to South Korea, Seoul should not rely on this commitment to deter aggression at low levels of conflict, nor on overflights by nuclear-capable aircraft to reliably affect the regime's behavior. The U.S.-ROK alliance should maintain the capabilities necessary to conduct robust counter-SOF and antisubmarine operations at high readiness, as well as an enhanced network of sensors and intelligence assets to track North Korean assets in the littorals and airspace around North Korea and deep within the country itself. The Task Force strongly supports the deployment of Terminal High-Altitude Area Defense (THAAD) to supplement existing ballistic missile defense capabilities, and recommends that both countries be prepared to assist each other in mitigating the negative effects of potential reprisals for the deployment.

Second, the U.S. and South Korean armed forces should jointly cultivate resilience to cyberattacks, prepare to operate in an environment of degraded information awareness, and prepare to assist South Korean civilians who may be affected by these attacks.[106] Civilian officials should build on existing efforts to jointly develop plans to respond to different types of cyberattacks, readying differential responses to attacks against private industry, public utilities, government, and armed forces.[107]

Third, although it is not their intention to employ these capabilities preventively, the United States, in close coordination with its allies, is obliged to develop the ability to forcibly secure stocks of North Korean fissile material in the event of a war or regime collapse and to strike at the North Korean leadership in an emergency.[108]

VI. *The Task Force recommends that the United States, South Korea, and Japan build capacity to intercept all missile launches with a range-payload capability greater than existing Scud missiles originating from North Korea, whether they are declared to be ballistic missile tests or civil space launch vehicles. In the event that Pyongyang fails to reenter negotiations, or the negotiations fail, the three partners should be prepared to declare and then implement this policy.*

To delay or prevent North Korea from achieving confidence in its ability to strike the U.S. homeland, the United States should publicly initiate trilateral cooperation to prepare to intercept all missile launches with a range-payload capability greater than existing Scuds, whether the launch is declared to be a ballistic missile test or a civil space launch vehicle.[109] The United States and its allies should justify this action as a way of enforcing UN Security Council Resolution 1718 and subsequent resolutions, which North Korea has repeatedly violated by carrying out illegal tests of ballistic missiles.[110] Without a protracted and successful program to test the KN-08 or another ICBM and its associated reentry vehicle, Pyongyang will lack the capability to deliver a nuclear warhead with any confidence. Preventing this threshold from being crossed would both strengthen the hand of the U.S.-ROK-Japan partnership in controlling escalation on the peninsula and forestall a threat to the U.S. homeland. In announcing the policy, the partners should clearly specify that it applies only to North Korea's illegal missile program and should be accompanied by the described measures to deter and defend against any and all violent reprisals. If North Korea fails to accept the new offer for negotiations and abide by its associated preconditions, the three partners should implement this policy. The United States and its allies should explicitly reserve the right in any case to intercept any projectile that they consider an immediate kinetic threat to allied personnel, territory, or civilians.

Collectively, these recommendations aim to delay and deny North Korea's ability to carry out a nuclear strike on the continental United States with confidence and hedge against the possibility that it does attain this capability. The United States and its allies need to prepare to meet their national security requirements under any eventuality, including continued expansion of the North Korean missile and nuclear arsenal, to deter and defend against aggression at the nuclear level and at lower levels of escalation.

It is not currently the policy of the U.S. government to induce a collapse of the North Korean regime. However, if North Korea's nuclear capabilities continue to expand and it continues to refuse to negotiate, the U.S. administration will have to work with allies to reassess overall strategy toward the regime and consider more assertive military and political actions, including those that directly threaten the existence of the regime and its nuclear and missile capabilities.

Conclusion

A comprehensive agreement that creates a nuclear-free and morally tolerable North Korea has grown less likely each year. Yet a narrow margin remains. To achieve an agreement will require protracted, costly, and risky efforts to sharpen the choice North Korea faces—to offer greater inducements for cooperation and impose heightened costs for continued defiance. If the United States and its allies can convince China that cooperation over North Korea is in its best interests, it may be possible that China will help enforce new UN sanctions, compel North Korea back to the negotiating table, force it to remain until an acceptable solution is found, and then ensure that the terms are implemented. However, the United States cannot trust that this outcome will come to pass or wait for the situation to evolve of its own accord, particularly as the nuclear threat grows; it needs to be ready to defend its national security interests and those of its allies in the face of continued Chinese reticence and North Korean intransigence.

Either route requires that the United States prioritize North Korea as a critical national security issue. For too long, the difficulty of the problem has inhibited creative thinking and concerted attention, and the United States is currently paying a steep price measured in the safety of the U.S. homeland, the security of U.S. allies, and an aggravated relationship with a rising China. Prioritizing North Korea may mean incurring costs to other U.S. objectives, but the rising threat to regional stability and U.S. national security means that it cannot be overlooked. The impending nuclear threshold where the DPRK can strike the U.S. homeland with nuclear weapons, and evolving regional dynamics, may mean that the next U.S. president might have the last chance to end the North Korean threat and secure a stable, prosperous maritime Asia.

Additional and Dissenting Views

Of the many CFR Task Force reports on North Korea released over the past two decades, this one in my view is the most reasoned and realistic, and I am happy to endorse its general thrust.

I would also like to make four additional points:

1. Although there is obvious appeal to achieving a negotiated settlement with the DPRK to the many threats it poses to the United States, its allies, and the world, U.S. policymakers should recognize how exceedingly unlikely such an outcome is today—or ever can be, given the nature of the real, existing North Korean government. U.S. objectives are regarded in Pyongyang as existential threats to survival—and governments simply do not trade away their survival. It therefore verges on magical thinking to imagine that the United States' record of near-total failure in nuclear diplomacy with North Korea over the past generation can somehow be dramatically changed absent a change of negotiating partners in the DPRK.

2. The notion that we might achieve dramatically better negotiation outcomes with North Korea through "carefully and deliberately sequenced [steps] to calibrate pressure" and "credibly signal[ling]" is—let us speak plainly—a fanciful conceit. Our North Korean interlocutors did not take that game-theory course, and they do not respond like one's partners from that graduate school seminar on bargaining. Instead of straining to devise a perfectly calibrated menu of incentives and disincentives for bringing North Korea "back to the table," the United States should instead be concentrating on something tangible and manifestly in its interest: namely, threat reduction. Reducing North Korea's capacity to harm the United States and its allies does not require North Korean assent—Washington can do this unilaterally, irrespective of Pyongyang's inclination to parley with us. This indeed should be our top priority in North Korea policy.

3. U.S. policymakers should be very careful in discussing any possible "peace treaty" with North Korea. Do we actually understand why such a treaty has been a top priority of North Korean policy for over half a century? Pyongyang holds that the U.S.-ROK military alliance must end, and U.S. troops in the peninsula must leave, once such a document is signed. North Korea is not the only state longing for a reduced U.S. military presence in Northeast Asia. Russia is another. So is China. Incidentally, Americans ought to think long and hard about the potential unintended consequences of confiding to Beijing that "attenuation of the [North Korean] threat may allow for a commensurate reduction of U.S. force posture on the peninsula." We might be better served instead by explaining to Beijing that our alliance with the ROK is intended to deal with threats in the post-DPRK world, too.

4. Finally, let us be clear about the essence of the North Korean nuclear threat: that threat is the North Korean government itself. So long as the real existing North Korean government holds power, that threat will continue. It is therefore incumbent upon the United States and its allies to plan for a successful Korean reunification that does not include the DPRK.

Nicholas Eberstadt
joined by Mary Beth Long and Walter L. Sharp

We agree with the report's general recommendation that the United States and South Korea should make efforts to reassure China that Korean unification will not damage China's interests. However, we take issue with some of the specific proposals in this regard. Specifically, we do not believe that it is necessary and is instead potentially harmful to U.S. and alliance interests to "jointly develop and present to China conditions under which the alliance would consider revising the number and disposition of U.S. forces on the peninsula."

It is our view that providing such detailed reassurances to China right now would not incentivize Beijing to restrict North Korea's ability to threaten its neighbors, as the report maintains. More important, we believe that discussions about potential readjustments in force posture would undermine U.S. and South Korean interests. Any mention of possible troop reductions could create doubts among South Korean elites and the public about the U.S. commitment to their security and, thus, undermine domestic support in Korea for the U.S.-ROK alliance, while gaining little from China for doing so.

First and foremost, discussion about the future U.S. force posture, including U.S. troop reductions, should be conducted within the alliance and based on prevailing circumstances, not uncertain future projections. It would be unwise and counterproductive to speculate about how conditions on the Korean Peninsula might change and posit different postures based on different scenarios for the purpose of influencing Chinese policy. China is well aware that the U.S.-ROK alliance is intended to deter and respond to threats from North Korea. As part of a strategy of providing reassurances to China to assuage its concerns about unification, it would be sufficient to convey to Beijing that, should the North Korean threat disappear, the alliance would consider how to respond, and future U.S. force posture would be a part of that process—in close coordination and consultation with South Korea.

Bonnie S. Glaser and Evan S. Medeiros
joined by Victor D. Cha, Mary Beth Long, and Walter L. Sharp

I was honored to participate in this Task Force, and I hope this effort sparks debate about what steps our nation must soon take to change Pyongyang's policy of provocation and a rapidly advancing nuclear program, lest the United States face North Korea as an unpredictable nuclear power.

There is much to applaud in this report. Significantly, the Task Force acknowledges that for decades the United States has been trapped in an increasingly dangerous and unproductive cycle in which North Korea provokes a crisis to which the United States responds with demands for discussions and, ultimately, with concessions. To break this cycle, the Task Force endorses, among other things, a collective security commitment declaring that an attack against South Korea or Japan is an attack against all. It also suggests the United States and its allies adopt a policy to intercept North Korea's long-range missile launches, including tests. In addition, the report rightly recommends that Kim Jong-un's ruthless regime lose its United Nations credentials unless it demonstrates progress in respecting human rights.

Regrettably, some elements of this report undermine these recommendations. Although few would argue that a policy rejecting diplomacy is a wise one, fewer still can claim that years of diplomatic efforts
have resulted in any indication that Kim Jong-un is less intent on acquiring nuclear weapons. On the contrary, after decades of talks, North
Korea's tests have accelerated to an unprecedented pace. The failure of
the talks to change North Korean behavior should raise questions about
the effectiveness of negotiations as a precursor to other policy options,
particularly those designed to unequivocally raise the costs of North
Korean aggression.

Without understanding why we might expect different results from
renewed negotiations, policymakers might consider a more creative
approach to sequencing that entails long-overdue responses to North
Korean provocations, including powerful sanctions and intercepts. At
a minimum, talks should resume only if and when North Korea indi-
cates an interest in negotiation and China is willing to apply meaningful pressure for change. Moreover, restructuring talks on peripheral
issues while avoiding an unequivocal demand for a halt to nuclear testing should be viewed as a dangerous return to the status quo. Even as a
threshold state only, North Korea still would be an impermissible threat
to our allies. And Iran and other nuclear aspirants are watching.

The report also lacks an appropriate sense of urgency. According to
the Director of National Intelligence, Pyongyang now "tops the list" of
nuclear and proliferation threats. Soon after Kim Jung-un took power,
hard-to-find, Chinese-designed mobile missile launchers were discov-
ered with weaponry that could reach U.S. bases in Japan. The DPRK
also is developing a submarine-launched ballistic missile capable of
reaching the continental United States. In addition, North Korea is
reportedly expanding its uranium enrichment facility at Yongbyon,
and has successfully launched a satellite with a three-stage rocket that, if
reconfigured, could reach the West Coast. The question now is whether
a new U.S. president must set limits beyond which the North Korean
nuclear program may not go.

Mary Beth Long
joined by Walter L. Sharp

I strongly agree with the policy thrusts and sequenced strategy recommendations reached by the group. However, in Recommendations II

and VI, I believe the conditions for ending talks with North Korea are not comprehensive enough and the concessions suggested during talks are offered prematurely.

Recommendation II states, "The United States should undertake talks subject to the following conditions . . . a moratorium on tests of nuclear weapons and missiles with a range-payload capability greater than existing Scud missiles." I believe the condition should include all ballistic missile tests governed by current UN Security Council resolutions. Short and intermediate tests threaten South Korea, Japan, and Guam. They also increase the knowledge needed to obtain a long-range missile capability. I also believe this condition needs to include a moratorium of all kinetic and cyberattacks on South Korea, Japan, and the United States. Additionally, Recommendation VI states, "The United States, South Korea, and Japan [should] build capacity to intercept all missile launches with a range-payload capability greater than existing Scud missiles originating from North Korea." Again, I do not believe this intercept capability should be limited to long-range missiles. The ROK and Japan need to develop a capability to defeat *all* missiles and rockets launched from North Korea in order to protect both military and population centers. Bottom line is the United States should cut off talks if North Korea attacks with any means, and the U.S.-ROK alliance needs an airtight capability to defeat all North Korea missiles and rockets.

Recommendation II also states, "Parties may explore steps on conventional arms control (including limits to the deployment of and exercises with [U.S. and ROK] conventional forces)." I do not believe we should consider this concession until we have verified that North Korea has completely eliminated its nuclear and missile capability and that this elimination is irreversible. ROK and U.S. deployments and exercises are designed to deter North Korea and prepare to defend if deterrence fails. Until the threat is eliminated, we should not reduce our preparedness. Further, until North Korea becomes a nation that abides by international norms and has granted its citizens the human rights they deserve, a collapse and regime change is possible. We should increase, not decrease, deployment and exercises that prepare the alliance for instability in North Korea.

In summary, we should agree to talks with North Korea, but only if it stops all provocations and agrees to and rapidly moves toward a nuclear-free peninsula. Unfortunately, history shows that North Korea has never lived up to these conditions. Therefore, we must maintain the

U.S.-ROK alliance's ability to deter and defend against North Korean actions and attacks.

Walter L. Sharp
joined by Mary Beth Long

While I concur with and fully endorse the findings and recommendations of the report, I do not believe that the Task Force's final recommendation to "strengthen deterrence and defense" goes far enough with respect to the actual consequences of further North Korean nuclear weapons and long-range missile development. The Kim Jong-un regime is continuing its aggressive effort to develop and deploy a long-range, nuclear-capable missile, which will eventually enable the DPRK to hold at risk the western continental United States. While this does not, in itself, constitute an existential threat, it does represent a sufficiently grave danger to U.S. interests and to the population of the western United States that it cannot go unchallenged, much less be tolerated.

It appears, at this point, inevitable that North Korea will soon achieve (if it has not already) sufficient miniaturization and hardening of its nuclear warhead design to facilitate successful launch and reentry atop an intercontinental missile. Thus, it is my personal view that if the DPRK continues to test and moves to deploy a missile system capable of ranging the continental United States, the U.S. government should respond by stating unequivocally that *any* evidence of preparations to make such a system operational would constitute a serious and unacceptable threat to U.S. national security and would immediately make all such missile launch sites a legitimate target for U.S. military force.

Given the apparent North Korean determination to move ahead with deploying a long-range missile—and, quite possibly, with additional nuclear tests intended, in part, to confirm successful miniaturization—I think it is essential for the United States to be *explicit* about its intentions in the event that DPRK were to move ahead with efforts to induct a nuclear-capable ICBM system.

Mitchel B. Wallerstein
joined by Mary Beth Long and Walter L. Sharp

Endnotes

1. For a summary of recent diplomacy, see Stephan Haggard, "Diplomatic Update," North Korea: Witness to Transformation (blog), Peterson Institute for International Economics, June 22, 2016, http://piie.com/blogs/north-korea-witness-transformation/diplomatic-update-0.
2. There is no certainty when North Korea will cross the threshold. In April, 2016, the South Korean government determined that Pyongyang could mount a nuclear warhead on a medium-range missile. Choe Sang-Hun, "South Korea Says North Has Capacity to Put Nuclear Warhead on a Missile," *New York Times*, April 5, 2016, http://www.nytimes.com/2016/04/06/world/asia/north-korea-nuclear-warhead-rodong-missile.html.
3. Alastair Gale and Carol E. Lee, "U.S. Agreed to North Korea Peace Talks Before Latest Nuclear Test," *Wall Street Journal*, February 21, 2016, http://www.wsj.com/articles/u-s-agreed-to-north-korea-peace-talks-1456076019.
4. Choe Sang-Hun, "North Korea's Kim Jong-un Tells Military to Have Nuclear Warheads on Standby," *New York Times*, March 3, 2016, http://www.nytimes.com/2016/03/04/world/asia/north-koreas-kim-jong-un-tells-military-to-have-nuclear-warheads-on-standby.html.
5. The canonical history of North-South relations can be found in Don Oberdorfer, *The Two Koreas: A Contemporary History* (New York: Basic Books, 2013). For a critical look at the cycle of provocation, see Van Jackson, *Rival Reputations: Coercion and Credibility in US-North Korea Relations* (Cambridge: Cambridge University Press, 2016).
6. For recent thinking on the possibility of collapse, see Bruce W. Bennett and Jennifer Lind, "The Collapse of North Korea: Military Missions and Requirements," International Security 36, no. 2, October 2011, pp. 84–119; Bruce W. Bennett, "Preparing for the Possibility of a North Korean Collapse" (Santa Monica: Rand Corporation, 2013), http://www.rand.org/content/dam/rand/pubs/research_reports/RR300/RR331/RAND_RR331.pdf; Bruce E. Bechtol, *North Korea and Regional Security in the Kim Jong-Un Era: A New International Security Dilemma* (London: Palgrave Macmillan, 2014).
7. Ken E. Gause, "North Korean House of Cards: Leadership Dynamics Under Kim Jong-un," Committee for Human Rights in North Korea, 2015, http://www.hrnk.org/uploads/pdfs/Gause_NKHOC_FINAL_WEB.pdf. In February 2016, the regime reportedly executed Ri Yong-gil, chief of the Korean People's Army General Staff. Yonhap News Agency, "N. Korea's Military Chief Executed on Corruption Charges: Sources," February 10, 2016, http://english.yonhapnews.co.kr/northkorea/2016/02/10/50/0401000000AEN20160210005051315F.html.
8. Nicholas Eberstadt, "North Korea's 'Epic Economic Fail' in International Perspective," Asan Institute for Policy Studies, November 2015, http://www.aei.org/publication/north-koreas-epic-economic-fail-in-international-perspective/.

9. Hazel Smith, *North Korea: Markets and Military Rule* (Cambridge: Cambridge University Press, 2015); Marcus Noland, "Why Is North Korea Growing?" North Korea: Witness to Transformation (blog), Peterson Institute for International Economics, October 20, 2015, http://blogs.piie.com/nk/?p=14552; Eric Talmadge, "North Korea's Creeping Economic Reforms Show Signs of Paying Off," *Guardian*, March 5, 2015, http://www.theguardian.com/world/2015/mar/05/north-korea-economic-reforms-show-signs-paying-off; Anna Fifield, "North Korea's Growing Economy—and America's Misconceptions About It," *Washington Post*, March 13, 2015, http://www.washingtonpost.com/world/asia_pacific/north-koreas-growing-economy-and-americas-misconceptions-about-it/2015/03/13/b551d2d0-c1a8-11e4-a188-8e4971d37a8d_story.html.

10. Nat Ketchum and Jane Kim, "A Quiet Opening: North Koreans in a Changing Media Environment," InterMedia, http://www.intermedia.org/wp-content/uploads/2013/05/A_Quiet_Opening_FINAL_InterMedia.pdf.

11. Yonho Kim, "Cell Phones in North Korea," US-Korea Institute at SAIS, 2014, http://uskoreainstitute.org/wp-content/uploads/2014/03/Kim-Yonho-Cell-Phones-in-North-Korea.pdf; "North Korea Media and IT Infrastructure Report," North Korea Strategy Center, 2015, http://en.nksc.co.kr/wp-content/uploads/2015/08/NKSC-North-Korea-Media-and-IT-Infrastructure-Report.pdf.

12. For more on the history of the China-DPRK relationship, see Jonathan D. Pollack, *No Exit: North Korea, Nuclear Weapons, and International Security* (London: International Institute for Strategic Studies, 2011).

13. Jonathan D. Pollack, "China and North Korea: The Long Goodbye?" Order from Chaos (blog), Brookings Institution, March 28, 2016, http://www.brookings.edu/blogs/order-from-chaos/posts/2016/03/28-china-north-korea-sanctions-pollack.

14. BBC News, "China Restricts North Korea Trade Over Nuclear Tests," April 5, 2016, http://www.bbc.com/news/world-asia-35969412. For one recent example, see Elizabeth Shim, "China, North Korea Exchange War of Words Through Media," United Press International, April 8, 2016, http://www.upi.com/Top_News/World-News/2016/04/08/China-North-Korea-exchange-war-of-words-through-media/9191460137544/.

15. China later denied the deployment. See Ben Blanchard, "China Denies Rushing Forces to Border During Korean Tensions," Reuters, August 27, 2015, http://www.reuters.com/article/us-china-northkorea-idUSKCN0QW12Y20150827; Van Jackson and Adam Mount, "An Opening on North Korea?" *National Interest*, November 2, 2015, http://nationalinterest.org/feature/opening-north-korea-14225; and Jane Perlez, "Mystery Cloaks a North Korean Pop Band's Canceled Beijing Dates," December 21, 2015, http://www.nytimes.com/2015/12/22/world/asia/north-korea-china-moranbong.html.

16. For this abortive effort, see Morgan Winsor, "China-North Korea Relations: Will Kim Jong-Un Visit Xi Jinping in Beijing?" *International Business Times*, October 13, 2015, http://www.ibtimes.com/china-north-korea-relations-will-kim-jong-un-visit-xi-jinping-beijing-2139030.

17. China Radio International Online, "China to Never Allow War or Chaos on Korean Peninsula: Xi," April 28, 2016, http://en.people.cn/n3/2016/0428/c90000-9051184.html.

18. Andrea Berger, "From Paper to Practice: The Significance of New UN Sanctions on North Korea," *Arms Control Today*, May 2016, http://www.armscontrol.org/ACT/2016_05/Features/From-Paper-to-Practice-The-Significance-of-New-UN-Sanctions-on-North-Korea.

19. Paul Boutin, "Is China Cutting Off North Korea? New Analysis of Satellite Images Say No," Medium.com, July 26, 2016, http://medium.com/planet-stories/is-china-cutting-off-north-korea-new-analysis-of-satellite-images-say-no-bd7cccb2143#.dr5071fs5;

Jeffrey Lewis, "No, China Isn't Punishing North Korea," Armscontrolwonk.com, July 26, 2016, http://www.armscontrolwonk.com/archive/1201736/no-china-isnt-punishing-north-korea/. For an alternative view, see Beyond Parallel, "Images Suggest Decrease in Sino-NK Border Trade," Center for Strategic and International Studies, July 1, 2016, http://beyondparallel.csis.org/decrease-in-trade-after-nuclear-test/; Josh Rogin, "Satellite Imagery Suggests China Is Secretly Punishing North Korea," *Washington Post*, July 1, 2016, http://www.washingtonpost.com/opinions/global-opinions/satellite-imagery-suggests-china-is-secretly-punishing-north-korea/2016/06/30/8638d8d6-3ee8-11e6-80bc-d06711fd2125_story.html.

20. Elizabeth Shim, "Top North Korea Official Ri Su Yong in Beijing to Boost Cooperation," United Press International, May 31, 2016, http://www.upi.com/Top_News/World-News/2016/05/31/Top-North-Korea-official-Ri-Su-Yong-in-Beijing-to-boost-cooperation/9201464707248/. For the nuclear remarks, see Jane Perlez, "North Korea Tells China of 'Permanent' Nuclear Policy," *New York Times*, May 31, 2016, http://www.nytimes.com/2016/06/01/world/asia/china-north-korea-ri-su-yong.html.

21. Jenny Jun, Scott LaFoy, and Ethan Sohn, "North Korea's Cyber Operations: Strategy and Responses," Center for Strategic and International Studies, December 2, 2015, http://csis.org/files/publication/151216_Cha_NorthKoreasCyberOperations_Web.pdf; Taylor Brooks, "Why China Needs to Rein In North Korea's Hackers," *Christian Science Monitor*, February 5, 2016, http://www.csmonitor.com/World/Passcode/Passcode-Voices/2016/0205/Opinion-Why-China-needs-to-rein-in-North-Korea-s-hackers.

22. Choe Sang-Hun, "Japan and South Korea Settle Dispute Over Wartime 'Comfort Women,'" *New York Times*, December 28, 2015, http://www.nytimes.com/2015/12/29/world/asia/comfort-women-south-korea-japan.html.

23. Michael Auslin, "A New Era in South Korean-Japanese Relations Begins," American Enterprise Institute, December 30, 2015, https://www.aei.org/publication/a-new-era-in-south-korean-japanese-relations-begins/.

24. "Trilateral Information Sharing Arrangement Concerning the Nuclear and Missile Threats Posed by North Korea Among the Ministry of National Defense of the Republic of Korea, the Ministry of Defense of Japan, and the Department of Defense of the United States of America," U.S. Department of Defense, December 29, 2014, http://archive.defense.gov/pubs/Trilateral-Information-Sharing-Arrangement.pdf. KJ Kwon and Dugald McConnell, "South Korea, Japan to Join U.S. Missile-Defense Exercise," CNN.com, May 17, 2016, http://www.cnn.com/2016/05/16/asia/south-korea-japan-missile-defense-exercise/.

25. Victor Cha, "Path Less Chosun," *Foreign Affairs*, October 8, 2015, http://www.foreignaffairs.com/articles/china/2015-10-08/path-less-chosun; for an earlier such effort, see Sam King and Ting Shi, "Xi, Park Urge Resuming Talks on North Korea Nuke Program," *Bloomberg Business*, July 3, 2014, http://www.bloomberg.com/news/articles/2014-07-02/xi-arrival-in-south-korea-marked-by-north-korean-missile-tests.

26. Elizabeth Shim, "South Korea, China Oppose North Korea's Nuclear Program in Joint Statement," United Press International, September 2, 2015, http://www.upi.com/Top_News/World-News/2015/09/02/South-Korea-China-oppose-North-Koreas-nuclear-program-in-joint-statement/7331441208150/.

27. Ministry of Foreign Affairs of the People's Republic of China, "Xi Jinping Meets With President Park Geun-hye of ROK," April 1, 2016, http://www.fmprc.gov.cn/mfa_eng/zxxx_662805/t1353045.shtml. Kim Deok-hyun, "Nuclear Envoys From S. Korea, China Hold Talks on N. Korea," Yonhap News Agency, June 8, 2016, http://english.yonhapnews.co.kr/national/2016/06/08/74/0301000000AEN20160608009800315F.html.

28. Mark Fitzpatrick, "Leap Day in North Korea," *Foreign Policy*, February 29, 2012, http://foreignpolicy.com/2012/02/29/leap-day-in-north-korea/.

29. Emma Chanlett-Avery, Ian E. Rinehart, and Mary Beth D. Nikitin, "North Korea: U.S. Relations, Nuclear Diplomacy, and Internal Situation," CRS Report R41259, January 15, 2016, https://www.fas.org/sgp/crs/nuke/R41259.pdf.

30. Jane Perlez, "North Korea Tells China of 'Permanent' Nuclear Policy." See also Eric Talmadge, "North Korea: We Won't Abandon Nukes With US Gun to Our Head," Associated Press, June 24, 2016, http://bigstory.ap.org/article/2db82c19afc844cd976 9085bbed84da6/north-korea-we-wont-abandon-nukes-us-gun-our-head.

31. Kim Deok-hyun, "N. Korean Nuclear Envoy Says Six-Party Talks Are 'Dead,'" Yonhap News Agency, June 22, 2016, http://english.yonhapnews.co.kr/national/2016/06/22/5 2/0301000000AEN20160622010400315F.html.

32. Alastair Gale and Carol E. Lee, "U.S. Agreed to North Korea Peace Talks Before Latest Nuclear Test," *Wall Street Journal*, February 21, 2016, http://www.wsj.com/articles/u-s-agreed-to-north-korea-peace-talks-1456076019.

33. Colleen McCain Nelson and Kwanwoo Jun, "Obama Expresses Skepticism Over North Korean Offer," *Wall Street Journal*, April 24, 2016, http://www.wsj.com/articles/merkel-expresses-concern-over-syria-after-meeting-with-obama-1461514013.

34. For a perspective on the recent history of negotiations, see Leon V. Sigal, "Getting What We Need With North Korea," *Arms Control Today*, April 2016, http://www.armscontrol.org/ACT/2016_04/Features/Getting-What-We-Need-With-North-Korea.

35. Megan Cassella and Doina Chiacu, "U.S. Rejected North Korea Peace Talks Offer Before Nuclear Test: State Department," Reuters, February 22, 2015, http://www.reuters.com/article/us-northkorea-nuclear-idUSKCN0VU0XE.

36. Scott Snyder, "North Korea's Denuclearization: Is It Possible?" *Forbes*, November 19, 2015, http://www.forbes.com/sites/scottasnyder/2015/11/19/north-koreas-denuclearization-is-it-possible/.

37. Scott Snyder, "Addressing North Korea's Nuclear Problem," Council on Foreign Relations, November 19, 2015, http://www.cfr.org/north-korea/addressing-north-koreas-nuclear-problem/p37258; and James M. Acton, "Focus on Nonproliferation—Not Disarmament—in North Korea," Carnegie Endowment for International Peace, February 14, 2013, http://carnegieendowment.org/2013/02/14/focus-on-nonproliferation-not-disarmament-in-north-korea.

38. Roberta Cohen "Human Rights in North Korea: Addressing the Challenges," *International Journal of Korean Unification Studies* 22, no. 2, December 2013, pp. 29–62. http://www.hrnk.org/uploads/pdfs/RCohen_north_korea_Dec2013.pdf.

39. United Nations, United Nations Human Rights Council, "Report of the Commission of Inquiry on Human Rights in the Democratic People's Republic of Korea," A/HRC/25/63, February 7, 2014, p. 6, http://www.ohchr.org/EN/HRBodies/HRC/RegularSessions/Session25/Documents/A-HRC-25-63_en.doc.

40. Ibid., 14.

41. Ibid., 7.

42. Ibid., 12.

43. For a list of human rights treaties that count North Korea as a signatory, see "North Korea, International Treaties Adherence," Rule of Law in Armed Conflicts Project, Geneva Academy of International Humanitarian Law and Human Rights, October 2010. http://www.geneva-academy.ch/RULAC/international_treaties.php?id_state=50.

44. "South Korea Questions North Korea's Qualifications as U.N. Member," *Korea Times*, February 19, 2016. http://www.koreatimes.co.kr/www/news/nation/2016/02/485_198416.html.

45. Elizabeth Shim, "North Korea Defends Human Rights Record Ahead of U.N. Meeting," United Press International, September 10, 2015, http://www.upi.com/Top_News/World-News/2015/09/10/North-Korea-defends-human-rights-record-ahead-of-UN-meeting/3581441909773/?src=r.

46. Lee Yeon Cheol, "Official: UN, N. Korea Discuss Possible Human Rights Visit," Voice of America, October 29, 2015, http://www.voanews.com/content/un-north-korea-discuss-possible-human-rights-visit/3028431.html.

47. Matt Sciavenza, "North Korea's Unsuccessful Charm Offensive," *Atlantic*, November 17, 2014, http://www.theatlantic.com/international/archive/2014/11/north-koreas-charm-offensive-un-international-criminal-court/382849/.

48. "UN Security Council Resolutions on North Korea," Arms Control Association, March 2016, http://www.armscontrol.org/factsheets/UN-Security-Council-Resolutions-on-North-Korea.

49. Andrea Berger, "Target Markets: North Korea's Military Customers," Whitehall Papers 84, no. 1, December 14, 2015, http://www.tandfonline.com/toc/rwhi20/84/1#.VtyYK_nSd4p.

50. United Nations, Security Council, "Report of the Panel of Experts Established Pursuant to Resolution 1874 (2009)," S/2016/157, February 24, 2016, http://www.un.org/ga/search/view_doc.asp?symbol=s/2016/157; Joshua Stanton, "Arsenal of Terror: North Korea, State Sponsor of Terrorism," Committee for Human Rights in North Korea, April 27, 2015, https://www.hrnk.org/uploads/pdfs/4_27_15_Stanton_ArsenalofTerror.pdf.

51. Paul K. Kerr, Mary Beth D. Nikitin, and Steven A. Hildreth, "Iran-North Korea-Syria Ballistic Missile and Nuclear Cooperation," CRS Report to Congress R43480, April 16, 2014, http://fpc.state.gov/documents/organization/225867.pdf; Joshua Pollack, "Ballistic Trajectory: The Evolution of North Korea's Ballistic Missile Market," *Nonproliferation Review* 18, no. 2, July 2011, pp. 411–29, http://www.nonproliferation.org/wp-content/uploads/npr/npr_18-2_pollack_ballistic-trajectory.pdf.

52. Joshua Stanton, "North Korea: The Myth of Maxed-Out Sanctions," *Fletcher Security Review* 2, no. 1, January 21, 2015, http://www.fletchersecurity.org/#!stanton/c1vgi; Bruce Klingner, "Time to Get North Korean Sanctions Right," Heritage Foundation, November 4, 2013, http://www.heritage.org/research/reports/2013/11/time-to-get-north-korean-sanctions-right.

53. White House, "Imposing Additional Sanctions With Respect to North Korea," Executive Order 13687, January 2, 2016. https://www.whitehouse.gov/the-press-office/2015/01/02/executive-order-imposing-additional-sanctions-respect-north-korea.

54. North Korea Sanctions and Policy Enhancement Act of 2016, HR 757, 114th Cong. (2016), http://www.congress.gov/114/bills/hr757/BILLS-114hr757ih.pdf.

55. U.S. Department of the Treasury, "Treasury Takes Actions to Further Restrict North Korea's Access to the U.S. Financial System," press release, June 1, 2016, http://www.treasury.gov/press-center/press-releases/Pages/jl0471.aspx.

56. United Nations Security Council, Resolution 2270, S/RES/2270, March 2, 2016, http://www.mofa.go.jp/files/000149964.pdf.

57. Andrea Berger, "The New UNSC Sanctions Resolution on North Korea: A Deep Dive Assessment," *38 North*, March 2, 2016, http://38north.org/2016/03/aberger030216/; Richard Nephew, "UN Security Council's New Sanctions on the DPRK," *38 North*, March 2, 2016, http://38north.org/2016/03/rnephew030216/.

58. White House, "National Security Strategy, 2015," February 2015, http://www.whitehouse.gov/sites/default/files/docs/2015_national_security_strategy.pdf.

59. Joel S. Wit and Young Ahn Sun, "North Korea's Nuclear Futures: Technology and Strategy," US-Korea Institute at SAIS, 2015, http://38north.org/wp-content/

uploads/2015/02/NKNF-NK-Nuclear-Futures-Wit-0215.pdf; Mitchel B. Wallerstein, "The Price of Inattention: A Survivable North Korean Nuclear Threat?" *Washington Quarterly* 38, no. 3, November 4, 2015, pp. 21–35, http://twq.elliott.gwu.edu/sites/twq. elliott.gwu.edu/files/downloads/TWQ_Fall2015_Wallerstein.pdf.

60. Anna Fifield, "North Korea Says It Can Fit Nuclear Warheads on Ballistic Missiles," *Washington Post,* March 8, 2016. http://www.washingtonpost.com/ world/south-korea-imposes-new-sanctions-on-north-tells-pyongyang-it-must-change/2016/03/08/15b0d29e-490a-4697-9742-3c81dde5eb5f_story.html.

61. Yonhap News Agency, "N. Korea to 'Soon' Conduct Nuke Warhead, Ballistic Missile Tests," March 15, 2016, http://english.yonhapnews.co.kr/northkorea/2016/03/15/0401 000000AEN20160315001400320.html.

62. For public debate over miniaturization, see David E. Sanger, "US Commander Sees Key Nuclear Step by North Korea," *New York Times*, October 24, 2014, http://www. nytimes.com/2014/10/25/world/asia/us-commander-sees-key-nuclear-step-by-north-korea.html; and Jeffrey Lewis, "North Korea's Nuclear Weapons: The Great Miniaturization Debate," *38 North*, February 5, 2015, http://38north.org/2015/02/ jlewis020515/.

63. For an analysis of the KN-08, see John Schilling, "A Revised Assessment of the North Korean KN-08 ICBM," *Science & Global Security* 21 (2013): pp. 210–36.

64. On the submarine-launched ballistic missile tests, see John Schilling, "A New Submarine-Launched Ballistic Missile for North Korea," *38 North*, April 26, 2016, http://38north.org/2016/04/jschilling042516/; on the new MLRS artillery system, see Anna Fifield, "North Korea Has New Rocket System That Could Strike Seoul This Year, South Korea Warns," *Washington Post*, April 6, 2016, http://www.washingtonpost. com/world/south-korea-says-north-has-large-caliber-rocket-system-could-strike-seoul-this-year/2016/04/06/38cd0f52-fbce-11e5-a569-2c9e819c14e4_story.html; for the ICBM engine test, see John Schilling, "North Korea's Large Rocket Engine Test: A Significant Step Forward for Pyongyang's ICBM Program," *38 North*, April 11, 2016, http://38north.org/2016/04/schilling041116/; on the satellite launch, see Michael Elleman, "North Korea Launches Another Large Rocket: Consequences and Options," *38 North*, February 10, 2016, http://38north.org/2016/02/mellemano21016/; on the failed Musudan IRBM test, see Anna Fifield, "North Korea's Missile Launch Has Failed, South's Military Says," *Washington Post*, April 15, 2016, http://www. washingtonpost.com/world/asia_pacific/north-koreas-missile-has-failed-officials-from-south-say/2016/04/14/8eb2ce53-bc38-40d0-9013-5655bed26764_story. html; on the successful test, see John Schilling, "A Partial Success for the Musudan," *38 North*, June 23, 2016, http://38north.org/2016/06/jschilling062316/.

65. David Albright and Serena Kelleher-Vergantini, "Plutonium, Tritium, and Highly Enriched Uranium Production at the Yongbyon Nuclear Site," Institute for Science and International Security, June 14, 2016, http://isis-online.org/uploads/isis-reports/ documents/Pu_HEU_and_tritium_production_at_Yongbyon_June_14_2016_ FINAL.pdf; Wit and Ahn, "North Korea's Nuclear Futures"; Albright and Kelleher-Vergantini, "Update on North Korea's Reactors, Enrichment Plant, and Possible Isotope Separation Facility," Institute for Science and International Security, February 1, 2016, http://isis-online.org/uploads/isis-reports/documents/Yongbyon_ January_2016_Update_Final.pdf.

66. Additionally, North Korea has reportedly restarted its 4MWth IRT research reactor using domestically produced uranium. David Albright and Serena Kelleher Vergantini, "North Korea's IRT Reactor: Has It Restarted? Is It Safe?" Institute for International Security, March 9, 2016. Warhead estimate available in Albright and Kelleher-Vergatini, "Plutonium, Tritium, and Highly Enriched Uranium Production at the Yongbyon Nuclear Site."

67. Jonathan Landay, David Brunnstrom, and Matt Spetalnick, "North Korea Restarts Plutonium Production for Nuclear Bombs – U.S. Official," Reuters, June 8, 2016, http://www.reuters.com/article/us-northkorea-nuclear-usa-exclusive-idUSKCN0YT2I1; Yonhap News Agency, "S. Korea Closely Watching N.K. Nuclear Activity With Serious Concern: Gov't," June 8, 2016, http://english.yonhapnews.co.kr/national/20 16/06/08/0301000000AEN20160608000451315.html.

68. For a perspective on China's assessment, see Jeremy Page and Jay Solomon, "China Warns North Korean Nuclear Threat Is Rising," *Wall Street Journal*, April 22, 2015, http://www.wsj.com/articles/china-warns-north-korean-nuclear-threat-is-rising-1429745706.

69. Kerr, Nikitin, and Hildreth, "Iran-North Korea-Syria Ballistic Missile and Nuclear Cooperation"; Justin McCurry, "North Korea 'Is Exporting Nuclear Technology,'" *Guardian*, May 28, 2010, http://www.theguardian.com/world/2010/may/28/north-korea-exporting-nuclear-technology.

70. Van Jackson, "Alliance Military Strategy in the Shadow of North Korea's Nuclear Futures," U.S.-Korea Institute at SAIS, September 2015, http://38north.org/wp-content/uploads/2015/09/NKNF-Jackson-Alliance-09151.pdf; Robert Carlin and Robert Jervis, "Nuclear North Korea: How Will It Behave?" U.S.-Korea Institute at SAIS, October 2015, http://38north.org/wp-content/uploads/2015/10/CarlinJervis-final.pdf.

71. Brad Roberts, *The Case for U.S. Nuclear Weapons in the 21st Century* (Stanford, CA: Stanford University Press, 2015), pp. 58–80.

72. Keir A. Lieber and Daryl G. Press, "The Next Korean War," *Foreign Affairs*, April 1, 2013, http://www.foreignaffairs.com/articles/north-korea/2013-04-01/next-korean-war; Elbridge Colby, "Nuclear Security in the Third Offset Strategy: Avoiding a Nuclear Blind Spot in the Pentagon's New Initiative," Center for a New American Security, February 2015, http://www.cnas.org/avoiding-nuclear-blindspot-offset-strategy#.V6zbzfkrK70; Adam Mount, "The Strategic Logic of Nuclear Restraint," *Survival* 57, no. 4 (July 22, 2015):pp. 53–76, http://www.tandfonline.com/doi/full/10.10 80/00396338.2015.1069991.

73. White House, "Blocking the Property of Certain Persons Engaging in Significant Malicious Cyber-Enabled Activities," Executive Order 13694, April 1, 2015. http://www.treasury.gov/resource-center/sanctions/Programs/Documents/cyber_eo.pdf.

74. For an extensive assessment, see Anthony H. Cordesman and Aaron Lin, "The Changing Military Balance in the Koreas and Northeast Asia," Center for Strategic and International Studies, June 2015, http://csis.org/files/publication/150325_Korea_Military_Balance.pdf.

75. Office of the Secretary of Defense, "Military and Security Developments Involving the Democratic People's Republic of Korea: Report to Congress," U.S. Department of Defense, January 2016, http://www.defense.gov/Portals/1/Documents/pubs/Military_and_Security_Developments_Involving_the_Democratic_Peoples_Republic_of_Korea_2015.PDF.

76. "North Korea Deploys 300 New MLRS Along Front Line: Sources," Yonhap News Agency, April 24, 2016, http://english.yonhapnews.co.kr/national/2016/04/24/43/03 01000000AEN20160424001100315F.html.

77. Agreement is growing in Washington that strategic patience has failed. For one recent view, see Joel S. Wit, "Trapped in No-Man's-Land: The Future of US Policy Toward North Korea," US-Korea Institute at SAIS, June 2016, http://38north.org/wp-content/uploads/2016/06/NKNF_Wit-2016-06.pdf.

78. Jim Walsh and John Park, "To Stop the Missiles, Stop North Korea, Inc.," *New York Times,* March 10, 2016, http://www.nytimes.com/2016/03/10/opinion/to-stop-the-missiles-stop-north-korea-inc.html.

79. In one proposal for a sustainable U.S. defense posture in East Asia, Andrew Krepinevich proposes cultivating anti-access/area-denial capabilities in allied states along the first island chain. Andrew F. Krepinevich Jr., "How to Deter China: The Case for Archipelagic Defense," *Foreign Affairs* 94, no. 2, 2015. For an alternative view, see Michael D. Swaine, "The Real Challenge in the Pacific," *Foreign Affairs* 94, no. 3, 2015.

80. Reuters, "South Korea's Park Seeks 5-Party Talks on North's Nuclear Program," January 21, 2016, http://www.reuters.com/article/us-northkorea-nuclear-park-idUSKCN0V009D; The U.S. Department of State's Special Representative for North Korea Policy, Sung Kim, supported the idea in testimony to the Senate Foreign Relations Committee. United States Senate Committee on Foreign Relations, "The Persistent North Korea Denuclearization and Human Rights Challenge," October 20, 2015, http://www.foreign.senate.gov/hearings/the-persistent-north-korea-denuclearization-and-human-rights-challenge_102015.

81. For an analysis of the humanitarian dimension of DPRK crisis scenarios, see Roberta Cohen, "Human Rights and Humanitarian Planning for Crisis in North Korea," *International Journal of Korean Studies,* Fall/Winter 2015, http://www.brookings.edu/~/media/research/files/articles/2016/02/18-human-rights-north-korea-cohen/roberta-cohen--nk--art-reunification.pdf.

82. See Oberdorfer, *The Two Koreas: A Contemporary History*; for a critical look at the cycle of provocation, see Jackson, *Rival Reputations*.

83. Joint Statement of the Fourth Round of the Six-Party Talks, September 18, 2005, http://www.state.gov/p/eap/regional/c15455.htm.

84. These conditions are broadly consistent with those listed in Sec. 402 of the North Korea Sanctions and Policy Enhancement Act of 2016, HR 757.

85. For an argument for prioritizing human rights in U.S. North Korea policy, see Dan Aum, Greg Scarlatoiu, and Amanda Mortwedt Oh, "Crimes Against Humanity in North Korea: The Case for U.S. Leadership and Action," Robert F. Kennedy Center for Justice and Human Rights, 2014, http://www.icasinc.org/2014/2014l/2014ldxa.pdf.

86. Spyros Blavoukos and Dimitris Bourantonis, "The Presidency of the UNGA and the Case of South Africa (1974)," in *Chairing Multilateral Negotiations: The Case of the United Nations* (New York: Routledge, 2011), pp.45–52; United Nations General Assembly, Resolution 3206, "Credentials of representatives to the twenty-ninth session of the General Assembly," September 30, 1974, https://documents-dds-ny.un.org/doc/RESOLUTION/GEN/NR0/738/09/IMG/NR073809.pdf?OpenElement.

87. United Nations General Assembly, Resolution 3207, "Relationship Between the United Nations and South Africa," September 30, 1974, http://documents-dds-ny.un.org/doc/RESOLUTION/GEN/NR0/738/09/IMG/NR073809.pdf?OpenElement.

88. For a discussion of the legal basis for this step, see Dan Ciobanu, "Credentials of Delegations and Representation of Member States at the United Nations," *International and Comparative Law Quarterly* 25, no. 2, April 1976, pp. 351–81; Alden Abbott, Filiberto Augusti, Peter Brown, and Elizabeth Rode, "The General Assembly, 29th Session: The Decredentialization of South Africa," *Harvard International Law Journal* 16, no. 3, Summer 1975, pp. 576–88.

89. United Nations General Assembly, Resolution 69/188, "Situation of Human Rights in the Democratic People's Republic of Korea," December 18, 2014, http://www.un.org/en/ga/search/view_doc.asp?symbol=A/RES/69/188; United Nations General Assembly, A/C.3/70/L.35, "Situation of Human Rights in the Democratic People's Republic of Korea," October 30, 2015, http://www.securitycouncilreport.org/atf/cf/%7B65BFCF9B-6D27-4E9C-8CD3-CF6E4FF96FF9%7D/a_c3_70_L35.pdf; Somini Sengupta, "United Nations Security Council Examines North Korea's Human Rights," *New York Times*, December 22, 2014, http://www.nytimes.com/2014/12/23/

world/asia/united-nations-security-council-examines-north-koreas-human-rights.html; Michelle Nichols, "China, Russia Fail to Stop U.N. Meeting on Rights in North Korea," Reuters, December 10, 2015, http://www.reuters.com/article/us-northkorea-rights-un-idUSKBN0TT2RU20151210.

90. Nick Cumming-Bruce, "U.N. Seeks Ways to Try North Koreans for Human Rights Abuses," New York Times, March 23, 2016, http://www.nytimes.com/2016/03/24/world/asia/un-seeks-ways-to-try-north-koreans-for-human-rights-abuses.html?_r=0.

91. UN News Centre, "New UN Office Opens in Seoul to Monitor Human Rights Issues in DPR Korea," June 23, 2015, http://www.un.org/apps/news/story.asp?NewsID=51223#.VxZiaPkrK71.

92. Ha-young Choi, "S. Korea Passes North Korean Human Rights Law," NK News, March 3, 2016, http://www.nknews.org/2016/03/s-korea-passes-north-korean-human-rights-law/.

93. United Nations Human Rights Council, Resolution A/HRC/31/L.25, "Situation of Human Rights in the Democratic People's Republic of Korea," March 21, 2016, http://ap.ohchr.org/documents/dpage_e.aspx?si=A/HRC/31/L.25.

94. For more on this exemption, see Stephan Haggard, "Once Again, Sanctions Enforcement," North Korea: Witness to Transformation (blog), Peterson Institute for International Economics, July 5, 2016, http://piie.com/blogs/north-korea-witness-transformation/once-again-sanctions-enforcement.

95. Material assistance may consist of equipment needed for inspection or compensation for services lost by severing illegal contracts with North Korean entities. Legal assistance could place pro bono advisors in member countries to assist with the complex process to bring domestic legal codes into compliance with international obligations, to ensure that countries have the legal authority act when the time comes. Technical assistance may include efforts to train and equip regional coast guards and port authorities.

96. Disciplining the behavior of member states is a primary function of all international institutions. See Robert O. Keohane, After Hegemony (Princeton, NJ: Princeton University Press, 1984); Barbara Koremenos, Charles Lipson, and Duncan Snidal, "The Rational Design of International Institutions," International Organization 55, no. 4, 2001.

97. For more information on PSI, see Mary Beth Nikitin, "Proliferation Security Initiative (PSI)," CRS Report to Congress RL34327, June 15, 2012, http://www.fas.org/sgp/crs/nuke/RL34327.pdf; Emma Belcher, "The Proliferation Security Initiative: Lessons for Using Nonbinding Agreements," International Institutions and Global Governance working paper, Council on Foreign Relations, July 2011, http://www.cfr.org/proliferation/proliferation-security-initiative/p25394.

98. U.S. Department of the Treasury, "Treasury Sanctions North Korean Senior Officials and Entities Associated with Human Rights Abuses," July 6, 2016, http://www.treasury.gov/press-center/press-releases/Pages/jl0506.aspx.

99. For example, in 2016, the European Union moved to impose additional sanctions on Burundi for human rights reasons. Robin Emmott, "EU Ready to Impose More Sanctions on Burundi," Reuters, February 15, 2016, http://www.reuters.com/article/idUSKCN0VO0XC/.

100. For more on China's role in enforcing DPRK sanctions, see "John S. Park, "The Key to the North Korean Targeted Sanctions Puzzle," Washington Quarterly 37, no. 3, Fall 2014, http://twq.elliott.gwu.edu/sites/twq.elliott.gwu.edu/files/downloads/Park_Fall2014.pdf.

101. Elias Groll, "Bank Thefts Show North Korea's Hacking Prowess," Foreign Policy, May 27, 2016, http://www.foreignpolicy.com/2016/05/27/bank-thefts-show-north-koreas-hacking-might/; Nicole Perlroth and Michael Corkery, "North Korea Linked to Digital Attacks on Global Banks," New York Times, May 26, 2016, http://www.nytimes.

com/2016/05/27/business/dealbook/north-korea-linked-to-digital-thefts-from-global-banks.html.

102. U.S. Department of State, "Trilateral Statement Japan, Republic of Korea, and the United States," December 6, 2010, http://www.state.gov/r/pa/prs/ps/2010/12/152431.htm.

103. For a provocative explanation of why U.S. alliances in Asia lack this level of formalism and permanence, see Christopher Hemmer and Peter J. Katzenstein, "Why Is There No NATO in Asia? Collective Identity, Regionalism, and the Origins of Multilateralism," *International Organization* 56, no. 3, 2002.

104. On the history and advantages of collective security declarations, see Charles A. Kupchan and Clifford A. Kupchan, "The Promise of Collective Security," *International Security* 20, no. 1, 1995.

105. In June 2016, NATO Secretary-General Jens Stoltenberg declared that a cyberattack could trigger Article 5, which mandates a collective response to an attack on a NATO member. Colin Clark, "NATO Declares Cyber a Domain," *Breaking Defense,* June 14, 2016, http://breakingdefense.com/2016/06/nato-declares-cyber-a-domain-nato-secgen-waves-off-trump/. See also Franklin D. Kramer, Robert J. Butler, and Catherine Lotrionte, "Cyber, Extended Deterrence, and NATO," Atlantic Council, May 2016, http://www.atlanticcouncil.org/images/publications/Cyber_Extended_Deterrence_and_NATO_web_0526.pdf. An overview of NATO's cyber policy is available at: North Atlantic Treaty Organization, "Cyber Defence," June 23, 2016, http://www.nato.int/cps/en/natohq/topics_78170.htm.

106. For more on North Korea's cyber capabilities and responses, see Jun, LaFoy, and Sohn, "North Korea's Cyber Operations."

107. Reginald Brothers and Jae-Yoo Choi, "Joint Statement of Intent Between the Department of Homeland Security Science and Technology Directorate, United States of America and the Ministry of Science, ICT, and Future Planning (MSIP), Republic of Korea," May 2, 2016, http://static.politico.com/e6/a1/08b6339f465ea51e2f87f1ec3e2e/us-south-korea-joint-cyber-agreement.pdf.

108. Anna Fifield, "In Drills, U.S., South Korea Practice Striking North's Nuclear Plants, Leaders," *Washington Post*, March 7, 2016, http://www.washingtonpost.com/world/in-drills-us-south-korea-practice-striking-norths-nuclear-plants/2016/03/06/46e6019d-5f04-4277-9b41-e02fc1c2e801_story.html.

109. For an ROK appraisal of the Scud-Extended Range, see Jeong Yong-soo and Kang Jin-kyu, "North's Scud-ER can reach U.S. base in Japan," *JoongAng Daily,* June 28, 2016, http://koreajoongangdaily.joins.com/news/article/article.aspx?aid=3020543.

110. United Nations Security Council, Resolution 1718, December 14, 2006, http://www.un.org/ga/search/view_doc.asp?symbol=S/RES/1718%282006%29.

Task Force Members

Task Force members are asked to join a consensus signifying that they endorse "the general policy thrust and judgments reached by the group, though not necessarily every finding and recommendation." They participate in the Task Force in their individual, not their institutional, capacities.

Victor D. Cha is a senior advisor and inaugural holder of the Korea chair at the Center for Strategic and International Studies (CSIS), as well as director of Asian studies and D.S. Song-KF chair at Georgetown University's Department of Government and School of Foreign Service. From 2004 to 2007, he served as director for Asian affairs at the White House on the National Security Council (NSC). Cha was also the deputy head of delegation for the United States at the Six Party Talks in Beijing and received two Outstanding Service Commendations during his tenure at the NSC. He is the award-winning author of *Alignment Despite Antagonism: The United States-Korea-Japan Security Triangle,* winner of the 2000 Ohira Book Prize; *Nuclear North Korea: A Debate on Engagement Strategies,* with Dave Kang; *Beyond the Final Score: The Politics of Sport in Asia; The Impossible State: North Korea, Past and Future,* selected by *Foreign Affairs* as a 2012 Best Book on Asia and the Pacific; and *Powerplay: Origins of the American Alliance System in Asia.* Cha is a former John M. Olin national security fellow at Harvard University, a two-time Fulbright Scholar, and a Hoover national fellow, CISAC fellow, and William J. Perry fellow at Stanford University. He holds Georgetown University's Dean's Teaching Award for 2010 and the Distinguished Research Award for 2011. He serves as an independent consultant and has testified before Congress on Asian security issues. Cha holds a BA, an MIA, and a PhD from Columbia University, as well as an MA from Oxford University.

Roberta Cohen is a specialist in human rights, humanitarian, and refugee issues and a leading expert on internally displaced persons and on human rights conditions in North Korea. For more than a decade, she was a senior fellow at the Brookings Institution and codirector of the Brookings Project on Internal Displacement together with the representative of the UN secretary-general on internally displaced persons. Together, they won the Grawemeyer Award for Ideas Improving World Order. She is co-chair emeritus of the Committee for Human Rights in North Korea, a distinguished group of foreign policy, human rights, and Asia experts; the author of more than one hundred articles and op-eds in the human rights field; a senior fellow at Georgetown University's Institute for the Study of International Migration; and a member of the committee on conscience of the U.S. Holocaust Memorial Museum. Earlier, she served as deputy assistant secretary of state for human rights and senior advisor to U.S. delegations to the UN Commission on Human Rights and General Assembly. She is a graduate of Barnard College and Johns Hopkins University's School of Advanced International Studies, and she received an honorary doctorate from the faculty of law at the University of Bern in Switzerland.

Joseph R. DeTrani is the president of Daniel Morgan Academy. He previously served as president of the Intelligence and National Security Alliance and now serves on their board of advisors. DeTrani was a former senior advisor to the director of national intelligence (DNI), director of the National Counter Proliferation Center, and intelligence community mission manager for North Korea. He also served at the U.S. Department of State as the special envoy for Six Party Talks with North Korea, and as the U.S. representative to the Korea Energy Development Organization. DeTrani had a distinguished career with the Central Intelligence Agency, serving as a member of the Senior Executive Service, director of East Asia operations, director for European operations, director of the office of technical services, director of public affairs, director of the crime and narcotics center, and executive assistant to Director of Central Intelligence William Casey. DeTrani served in the U.S. Air Force and is a graduate of New York University. He received a certificate in Chinese from the State Department Foreign Language School in Taiwan and attended Harvard University's International Security Program for executives. He has published numerous articles dealing with North Korea, China, Iran, cyber espionage, and nonproliferation issues.

Nicholas Eberstadt holds the Henry Wendt chair in political economy at the American Enterprise Institute in Washington, DC, and is a senior advisor to the National Bureau of Asian Research in Seattle. Eberstadt is an authority on issues of demography, development, and international security, and has published hundreds of articles in popular and scholarly journals on these topics over the course of the past four decades, as well as over twenty books and monographs. He has written extensively about North Korea; his studies include *The Population of North Korea* (coauthor), *The End of North Korea*, *The North Korean Economy Between Crisis and Catastrophe*, and *The North Korean Economy's "Epic Economic Fail" in International Perspective*. Eberstadt is a founding member of the U.S. Committee for Human Rights in North Korea. Previously, he has served as a member of the President's Council on Bioethics, the board of scientific counselors for the U.S. National Center for Health Statistics, and the World Economic Forum's Global Agenda Councils. He consults and advises with a range of offices within the U.S. government and has been invited to offer expert testimony before Congress on a wide range of issues. Eberstadt earned his AB, MPA, and a PhD at Harvard as well as an MSc from the London School of Economics.

Robert J. Einhorn is a senior fellow with the Brookings Institution's arms control and nonproliferation initiative. Before coming to Brookings in May 2013, Einhorn served as the U.S. Department of State's special advisor for nonproliferation and arms control, a position created by Secretary of State Hillary Clinton in 2009. Between 2001 and 2009, Einhorn was a senior advisor at the Center for Strategic and International Studies, where he directed the proliferation prevention program. Before coming to CSIS, he was assistant secretary of state for nonproliferation (1999–2001), deputy assistant secretary of state for political-military affairs (1992–99), and a member of the State Department Policy Planning Staff (1986–92). Between 1972 and 1986, he held various positions at the U.S. Arms Control and Disarmament Agency (ACDA), including as ACDA's representative to the strategic arms reduction talks with the Soviet Union. Einhorn holds a BA in government from Cornell University and a MA in public affairs and international relations from Princeton University's Woodrow Wilson School of Public and International Affairs.

Bonnie S. Glaser is a senior advisor for Asia and the director of the China power project at CSIS, where she works on issues related to Chinese foreign policy and U.S. security interests in Asia. She is concomitantly a nonresident fellow with the Lowy Institute in Sydney, Australia, a senior associate with CSIS Pacific Forum, and a consultant for the U.S. government on East Asia. From 2008 to mid-2015, Glaser was a senior advisor with the CSIS's Freeman chair in China studies, and from 2003 to 2008, she was a senior associate in the CSIS international security program. Prior to joining CSIS, she served as a consultant for various U.S. government offices, including the U.S. Departments of Defense and State. Glaser is a regular contributor to the Pacific Forum quarterly web journal *Comparative Connections*. She is currently a board member of the U.S. committee of the Council for Security Cooperation in the Asia Pacific, and a member of both the Council on Foreign Relations and the Institute of International Strategic Studies. She served as a member of the U.S. Department of Defense's Defense Policy Board China panel in 1997. Glaser received her BA in political science from Boston University and her MA with concentrations in international economics and Chinese studies from Johns Hopkins University's School of Advanced International Studies.

Mary Beth Long is a nonresident senior fellow at the Foundation for Defense of Democracies and was a senior subject matter expert to the supreme allied commander of NATO from 2013 to 2015. She is the founder and chief executive officer of Metis Solutions, recognized in 2014 by *Inc. Magazine's* 5,000 list as the 201st fastest-growing private company and the twelfth top government service company. She also consults for several Fortune 50 companies. Long was the first woman to be confirmed by the U.S. Senate as assistant secretary of defense in the Office of the Secretary of Defense (2007–2009), specifically as assistant secretary for international security affairs. Long chaired NATO's high-level group responsible for nuclear policy (2007–2009). She is a regular contributor to CNN, Bloomberg, Fox News, BBC, and NPR on foreign policy issues and the intelligence community. She is a licensed lawyer, and from 1999 until 2004 was an associate specializing in civil litigation matters at Williams & Connolly LLP. Long earned her JD from Washington and Lee University School of Law.

Catherine B. Lotrionte is the director and founder of the Cyber Project in Georgetown University's School of Foreign Service, where she teaches and writes on international and national security law, international affairs, and technology. In 2002, she was appointed by General Brent Scowcroft as counsel to the president's foreign intelligence advisory board at the White House, a position she held until 2006. In 2002, she served as a legal counsel for the joint inquiry committee of the Senate Select Committee on Intelligence, investigating the 9/11 terrorist attacks. Prior to that, Lotrionte was assistant general counsel in the Office of General Counsel at the Central Intelligence Agency and also served in the U.S. Department of Justice. She is an internationally recognized expert on international law and cyber conflict. Lotrionte holds an MA and a PhD from Georgetown University and a JD from New York University, and is the author of numerous publications, including two forthcoming books, *Cyber Policy: An Instrument of International Relations, Intelligence and National Power* and *U.S. National Security Law in the Post–Cold War Era.* She is a frequent speaker at cyber conferences worldwide and has founded and hosted the annual International Conference on Cyber Engagement at Georgetown University since 2011. Lotrionte currently serves on the World Economic Forum's Global Agenda Council on Cybersecurity and the CSIS cyber task force, and she is a member of the Council on Foreign Relations.

Evan S. Medeiros leads Eurasia Group's research on Asia. Most recently, he served as special assistant to the president and senior director for Asian affairs on the National Security Council, where he served as President Obama's top advisor on the Asia Pacific and coordinated U.S. policy in the region across the areas of diplomacy, defense policy, economic policy, and intelligence affairs. In 2009, he joined the NSC staff as director for China, Taiwan, and Mongolian affairs, and was actively involved in U.S.-China relations throughout his nearly six-year NSC tenure. From 2002 to 2009, Medeiros served as a senior political scientist at the RAND Corporation, specializing in research on the international politics of East Asia, China's foreign and national security policies, U.S.-China relations, and Chinese defense and security issues. From 2007 to 2008, he was policy advisor to the special envoy for China and the U.S.-China strategic economic dialogue at the Treasury Department, serving Secretary Henry Paulson. Prior to joining

RAND, Medeiros was a senior research associate at the Monterey Institute of International Studies, a visiting fellow at the Institute of American Studies at the China Academy of Social Sciences in Beijing, and an adjunct lecturer at China's Foreign Affairs College. He holds a PhD from the London School of Economics and Political Science, an MPhil from the University of Cambridge (where he was a Fulbright Scholar), an MA from the University of London's School of Oriental and African Studies, and a BA from Bates College in Maine. He travels to Asia frequently and speaks, reads, and writes Mandarin Chinese.

Adam Mount is a senior fellow at the Center for American Progress. Previously, he was a Stanton nuclear security fellow at the Council on Foreign Relations and prior to that worked on nuclear elimination contingencies at the RAND Corporation. Mount's writing has been published by *Foreign Affairs, Survival,* the *Nonproliferation Review, Democracy,* and other outlets. He is the coauthor with Lawrence J. Korb of the Center for American Progress report "Setting Priorities for Nuclear Modernization," the author of the Deep Cuts Commission working paper "Anticipatory Arms Control," and a columnist at the *Bulletin of the Atomic Scientists,* where he writes on nuclear strategy and force structure. He has spoken widely on strategic issues, including in testimony before the House Armed Services subcommittee on strategic forces. He holds a PhD in government from Georgetown University.

Mike Mullen is a retired U.S. Navy admiral who served as the seventeenth chairman of the Joint Chiefs of Staff. Mullen, who spent four years as chairman—the top military advisor to Presidents George W. Bush and Barack Obama—brought bold and original thinking to the work of strengthening the U.S. military and advocating for those who serve. Mullen oversaw the end of the combat mission in Iraq and the development of a new military strategy for Afghanistan, while promoting international partnerships, new technologies, and new counterterrorism tactics culminating in the killing of Osama bin Laden. A 1968 graduate from the U.S. Naval Academy in Annapolis, Mullen sought high-risk positions to develop his leadership skills. He served as chief of naval operations prior to assuming duties as chairman of the Joint Chiefs of Staff. Now retired from the U.S. Navy, Mullen serves on the boards of General Motors, Sprint, and the Bloomberg Family Foundation, and teaches at Princeton University's Woodrow Wilson School.

He is known for his honesty and candor, and for his efforts on behalf of service members, veterans, and their families.

Sam Nunn is co-chairman and chief executive officer of the Nuclear Threat Initiative (NTI). He served as a U.S. senator from Georgia for twenty-four years (1972–96). In addition to his work with NTI, Nunn has continued his service in the public policy arena as a distinguished professor in the Sam Nunn School of International Affairs at Georgia Tech and as chairman of the board of the Center for Strategic and International Studies in Washington, DC. Nunn attended Georgia Tech, Emory University, and Emory Law School, where he graduated with honors in 1962. After active duty service in the U.S. Coast Guard, he served six years in the U.S. Coast Guard Reserve. He first entered politics as a member of the Georgia House of Representatives in 1968. During his tenure in the U.S. Senate, Nunn served as chairman of the Senate Armed Services Committee and the permanent subcommittee on investigations. He also served on the intelligence and small business committees. His legislative achievements include the landmark Department of Defense Reorganization Act, drafted with the late Senator Barry Goldwater, and the Nunn-Lugar Cooperative Threat Reduction program, which provided assistance for more than twenty years to Russia and the former Soviet republics for securing and destroying their excess nuclear, biological, and chemical weapons.

Gary Samore is the executive director for research at the Belfer Center for Science and International Affairs at the Harvard Kennedy School. In December 2015, he was appointed as a member of the Secretary of Energy advisory board under Secretary Ernest Moniz. He is also a non-resident senior fellow at the Brookings Institution and member of the advisory board for United Against Nuclear Iran, a nonprofit organization that seeks to prevent Iran from acquiring nuclear weapons. He served for four years as President Obama's White House coordinator for arms control and weapons of mass destruction (WMD), including as U.S. sherpa for the 2010 Nuclear Security Summit in Washington, DC, and the 2012 Nuclear Security Summit in Seoul, South Korea. As WMD coordinator, he served as the principal advisor to the president on all matters relating to arms control and the prevention of WMD proliferation and terrorism, and coordinated U.S. government activities, initiatives, and programs to promote international arms control efforts.

Samore was a National Science Foundation fellow at Harvard University, where he received his MA and PhD in government in 1984. While at Harvard, he was a predoctoral fellow at what was then the Harvard Center for Science and International Affairs, later to become the Belfer Center for Science and International Affairs.

Walter L. Sharp graduated from West Point in 1974 and was commissioned an armor officer. He has earned a master of science degree in operations research and system analysis from Rensselaer Polytechnic Institute. Sharp commanded the United Nations Command, Republic of Korea – United States Combined Forces Command, and United States Forces Korea from June 3, 2008, to July 14, 2011. Earlier in his career, Sharp's command positions included: squadron commander, 1st Squadron, 7th U.S. Cavalry, 1st Cavalry Division, Fort Hood Texas; regimental commander, 2nd Armored Cavalry Regiment, Fort Polk, Louisiana; assistant division commander for maneuver 2nd Infantry Division, Camp Red Cloud, South Korea; and division commander, 3rd Infantry Division, Fort Stewart, Georgia. He commanded troops in Desert Shield and Desert Storm, Operation Uphold Democracy in Haiti, and SFOR's Multinational Division (North) in Bosnia. Sharp had four assignments at the Pentagon on the Joint Staff. He was the deputy director, J5 for Western Hemisphere/global transnational issues; vice director, J8 for force structure, resources, and assessment; director for strategic plans and policy, J5; and director of the Joint Staff. He is consulting for several U.S. and Korean companies; serves on the board of directors for NEXEO Solutions, ARTIS, and the Korea Society; and is involved in strategy and policy discussions at several DC-area think tanks concerning strategy and policy for Northeast Asia and especially Korea.

Mitchel B. Wallerstein was appointed as president of Baruch College of the City University of New York in August 2010. Baruch College is home to the nation's largest collegiate business school, the Zicklin School of Business, as well as prominent schools of arts and sciences and public affairs. From 2003 to 2010, he served as the dean of Syracuse University's Maxwell School of Citizenship and Public Affairs, which is the nation's number-one ranked graduate school of public and international affairs. Prior to leading the Maxwell School, Wallerstein was vice president of the John D. and Catherine T. MacArthur Foundation from 1998 to 2003, where he directed the foundation's international programs. Before that, he served from 1993 to 1998 as deputy assistant secretary of defense for counterproliferation policy and senior defense representative for trade security policy. During his five-year tenure, he dealt with nuclear, biological, and chemical weapons proliferation, as well as national security export controls; he also helped to found and subsequently co-chaired the senior defense group on proliferation at NATO. In January 1997, Secretary of Defense William J. Perry awarded Wallerstein the Secretary of Defense Medal for Outstanding Public Service, and he subsequently received the Bronze Palm to that award in April 1998. Wallerstein is a long-time member of the Council on Foreign Relations. In 2006, he was elected a fellow of the National Academy of Public Administration, and in 2015, he was similarly elected a fellow of the American Association for the Advancement of Science.

Robert F. Willard is president and chief executive officer of the Institute of Nuclear Power Operations. In May 2012, Willard completed a distinguished U.S. Navy career as the commander, U.S. Pacific Command, Camp H. M. Smith, Hawaii. Willard is a Los Angeles native and a 1973 graduate of the U.S. Naval Academy. He has a master's degree in engineering management from Old Dominion University and is an Massachusetts Institute of Technology Seminar XXI alumnus. An F-14 aviator, Willard served in a variety of West Coast fighter squadrons: VF-24, VF 124, VF-2, and VF-51 aboard the aircraft carriers USS *Constellation*, USS *Ranger*, USS *Kitty Hawk* and USS *Carl Vinson*. He was operations officer and executive officer of Navy Fighter Weapons School (TOPGUN). He later commanded the "Screaming Eagles" of Fighter Squadron 51. Following nuclear-power training, Willard served as executive officer of USS *Carl Vinson* (CVN 70), commanded the amphibious flagship USS *Tripoli* (LPH 10) in the Persian Gulf during "Operation Vigilant Warrior," for which Tripoli received a Navy Unit Commendation, and commanded the aircraft carrier USS *Abraham Lincoln* (CVN 72). As a flag officer, Willard twice served on the Joint Staff, was deputy and chief of staff for the U.S. Pacific Fleet, commanded Carrier Group Five aboard USS *Kitty Hawk* (CV 63), and commanded the U.S. Seventh Fleet. Willard became the thirty-fourth vice chief of naval operations in March 2005, assumed command of the U.S. Pacific Fleet in May 2007, and became the commander of U.S. Pacific Command in October 2009. His decorations include the Defense

Distinguished Service Medal, Distinguished Service Medal, Legion of Merit, and various other awards.

Juan Carlos Zarate is the chairman and cofounder of the Financial Integrity Network, the chairman and senior counselor for the Foundation for Defense of Democracies' Center on Sanctions and Illicit Finance, a visiting lecturer of law at the Harvard Law School, and the senior national security analyst for CBS News. He served as the deputy assistant to the U.S. president and deputy national security advisor for combating terrorism from 2005 to 2009, and was responsible for developing and implementing the U.S. government's counterterrorism strategy and policies related to transnational security threats. Zarate was the first assistant secretary of the Treasury for terrorist financing and financial crimes; he led domestic and international efforts to attack terrorist financing as well as the innovative use of the U.S. Treasury's national security-related powers. Zarate sits on several boards, including HSBC's financial system vulnerabilities committee, the Vatican's Financial Information Authority, and the board of advisors to the director of the National Counterterrorism Center. He is the author of *Treasury's War: The Unleashing of a New Era of Financial Warfare, Forging Democracy*, and a variety of articles.

Task Force Observers

Observers participate in Task Force discussions, but are not asked to join the consensus. They participate in their individual, not institutional, capacities.

Nate Adler is a professional staff member on the Senate Select Committee on Intelligence. He was formerly the defense and foreign policy advisor to Senator John D. Rockefeller IV and a Rosenthal fellow on the Senate Foreign Relations Committee, where he focused on U.S. foreign policy in East Asia. Adler received an MPA in international relations at Princeton University and an AM in East Asian studies at Harvard University. A San Francisco native, Adler is a term member at the Council on Foreign Relations and was a Fulbright Scholar to South Korea in 2005.

Patrick Costello is the director of Washington External Affairs at the Council on Foreign Relations in Washington, DC. In this capacity, he leads the Congress and U.S. Foreign Policy Program, CFR's diplomatic program and executive branch initiative, and regularly works with the policymaking community and the foreign diplomatic corps on a wide range of foreign policy and economic issues. Costello worked in Congress as an aide to former Representative Jon Porter, serving as the primary foreign policy and economic policy advisor. After leaving Capitol Hill, Costello was a government relations counselor with International Business-Government Counsellors where he directed congressional relations, and provided strategic advice, analysis, and direct representation. Prior to joining CFR's Washington office, he was a senior associate at the Whitaker Group, a consultancy and project development firm specializing in Africa. Originally from Boston, Massachusetts, Costello earned a bachelor's degree from the University of Massachusetts. He also earned a postgraduate certificate from Exeter College, University of Oxford, and a master's degree from King's College London. Costello has also done graduate study at the National Defense University. He was a 2011 Future Leader with the Foreign Policy Initiative, named an Atlantik-Brücke Young Leader in 2014, and is currently a term member of the Council on Foreign Relations.

Anya Schmemann (observer, ex officio) is Washington director of Global Communications and Media Relations and director of the Independent Task Force Program at the Council on Foreign Relations in Washington, DC. She recently returned to CFR after serving as assistant dean of communications and outreach at American University's School of International Service. Previously, Schmemann managed communications at the Belfer Center for Science and International Affairs at the Harvard Kennedy School and administered the Caspian studies program there. She coordinated a research project on Russian security issues at the EastWest Institute in New York and was assistant director of CFR's Center for Preventive Action in New York, focusing on the Balkans and Central Asia. She received a BA in government and an MA in Russian, East European, and Central Asian Studies, both from Harvard University. She was a Truman national security fellow and a nonresident senior fellow at the Center for the National Interest, and was a term member and is now a life member of the Council on Foreign Relations.

Sydney Seiler is the senior advisor on North Korea to the Office of the Director of National Intelligence. Prior to this position he served as the State Department special envoy for the Six Party Talks, where he coordinated U.S. efforts on denuclearization of North Korea through the Six Party Talks framework and led day-to-day negotiations with Six Party partners. Seiler served as the director for Korea on the National Security Council staff from April 2011 to August 2014. In that position, Seiler advised the president and senior White House officials on South and North Korea issues, and planned, directed, and coordinated policy on Korea. A member of the senior national intelligence service who has worked on Korean Peninsula issues for thirty-four years, Seiler served previously as the acting and deputy DNI national intelligence manager for North Korea, and had a variety of assignments across the intelligence community to include the Central Intelligence Agency and the National Security Agency. He participated in numerous rounds of Six Party Talks and bilateral U.S.-DPRK talks, and has served over twelve years in the Republic of Korea. Seiler received his MA degree in Korean studies from Yonsei University's Graduate School of International Studies and is a graduate of the Korean language programs of the Defense Language Institute and Yonsei University. He is the author of the book *Kim Il-Song 1941–1948: The Creation of a Legend, the Building of a Regime*, and is a recipient of the National Intelligence Superior Service Medal.

Sheila A. Smith, an expert on Japanese politics and foreign policy, is senior fellow for Japan studies at the Council on Foreign Relations. She is the author of *Intimate Rivals: Japanese Domestic Politics and a Rising China* and *Japan's New Politics and the U.S.-Japan Alliance*. Her current research focuses on how geostrategic change in Asia is shaping Japan's strategic choices. She joined CFR from the East-West Center in 2007 and was a visiting scholar at Keio University in 2007–2008, where she researched Japan's foreign policy toward China, supported by the Abe fellowship. Smith has been a visiting researcher at leading Japanese foreign and security policy think tanks and universities, including the Japan Institute of International Affairs, the Research Institute for Peace and Security, the University of Tokyo, and the University of the Ryukyus. Smith is vice chair of the U.S. advisors to the U.S.-Japan Conference on Cultural and Educational Interchange and serves on the advisory committee for the U.S.-Japan Network for the Future program run by the Maureen and Mike Mansfield Foundation. She teaches as an adjunct professor at Georgetown University and serves on the board of its *Journal of Asian Affairs*. She earned her MA and PhD degrees from the department of political science at Columbia University.

Scott Snyder is senior fellow for Korea studies and director of the program on U.S.-Korea policy at the Council on Foreign Relations, where he had served as an adjunct fellow from 2008 to 2011. Snyder's latest books include the coauthored volume *The Japan-South Korea Identity Clash: East Asian Security and the United States* and *Middle-Power Korea: Contributions to the Global Agenda*. Snyder is also the coeditor of *North Korea in Transition: Politics, Economy, and Society* and the editor of *Global Korea: South Korea's Contributions to International Security*. He served as the project director for CFR's Independent Task Force No. 64 on policy toward the Korean Peninsula. He currently writes for the CFR blog *Asia Unbound*. Prior to joining CFR, Snyder was a senior associate in the international relations program of the Asia Foundation, where he founded and directed the Center for U.S.-Korea Policy and served as the Asia Foundation's representative in Korea (2000–2004). He was also a senior associate at Pacific Forum CSIS. Snyder has worked as an Asia specialist in the research and studies program of the U.S. Institute of Peace and as acting director of Asia Society's contemporary affairs program. He was a Pantech visiting fellow at Stanford University's Shorenstein Asia-Pacific Research Center (2005–2006), and received an Abe fellowship, administered by the Social Sciences Research Council, from 1998 to 1999. Snyder received a BA from Rice University and an MA from the regional studies East Asia program at Harvard University, and was a Thomas G. Watson fellow at Yonsei University in South Korea.

Independent Task Force Reports

Published by the Council on Foreign Relations

Working With a Rising India: A Joint Venture for the New Century
Charles R. Kaye and Joseph S. Nye Jr., Chairs; Alyssa Ayres, Project Director
Independent Task Force Report No. 73 (2015)

The Emerging Global Health Crisis: Noncommunicable Diseases in Low- and Middle-Income Countries
Mitchell E. Daniels Jr. and Thomas E. Donilon, Chairs; Thomas J. Bollyky, Project Director
Independent Task Force Report No. 72 (2014)

North America: Time for a New Focus
David H. Petraeus and Robert B. Zoellick, Chairs; Shannon K. O'Neil, Project Director
Independent Task Force No. 71 (2014)

Defending an Open, Global, Secure, and Resilient Internet
John D. Negroponte and Samuel J. Palmisano, Chairs; Adam Segal, Project Director
Independent Task Force Report No. 70 (2013)

U.S.-Turkey Relations: A New Partnership
Madeleine K. Albright and Stephen J. Hadley, Chairs; Steven A. Cook, Project Director
Independent Task Force Report No. 69 (2012)

U.S. Education Reform and National Security
Joel I. Klein and Condoleezza Rice, Chairs; Julia Levy, Project Director
Independent Task Force Report No. 68 (2012)

U.S. Trade and Investment Policy
Andrew H. Card and Thomas A. Daschle, Chairs; Edward Alden and Matthew J. Slaughter, Project Directors
Independent Task Force Report No. 67 (2011)

Global Brazil and U.S.-Brazil Relations
Samuel W. Bodman and James D. Wolfensohn, Chairs; Julia E. Sweig, Project Director
Independent Task Force Report No. 66 (2011)

U.S. Strategy for Pakistan and Afghanistan
Richard L. Armitage and Samuel R. Berger, Chairs; Daniel S. Markey, Project Director
Independent Task Force Report No. 65 (2010)

U.S. Policy Toward the Korean Peninsula
Charles L. Pritchard and John H. Tilelli Jr., Chairs; Scott A. Snyder, Project Director
Independent Task Force Report No. 64 (2010)

U.S. Immigration Policy
Jeb Bush and Thomas F. McLarty III, Chairs; Edward Alden, Project Director
Independent Task Force Report No. 63 (2009)

U.S. Nuclear Weapons Policy
William J. Perry and Brent Scowcroft, Chairs; Charles D. Ferguson, Project Director
Independent Task Force Report No. 62 (2009)

Confronting Climate Change: A Strategy for U.S. Foreign Policy
George E. Pataki and Thomas J. Vilsack, Chairs; Michael A. Levi, Project Director
Independent Task Force Report No. 61 (2008)

U.S.-Latin America Relations: A New Direction for a New Reality
Charlene Barshefsky and James T. Hill, Chairs; Shannon O'Neil, Project Director
Independent Task Force Report No. 60 (2008)

U.S.-China Relations: An Affirmative Agenda, A Responsible Course
Carla A. Hills and Dennis C. Blair, Chairs; Frank Sampson Jannuzi, Project Director
Independent Task Force Report No. 59 (2007)

National Security Consequences of U.S. Oil Dependency
John Deutch and James R. Schlesinger, Chairs; David G. Victor, Project Director
Independent Task Force Report No. 58 (2006)

Russia's Wrong Direction: What the United States Can and Should Do
John Edwards and Jack Kemp, Chairs; Stephen Sestanovich, Project Director
Independent Task Force Report No. 57 (2006)

More than Humanitarianism: A Strategic U.S. Approach Toward Africa
Anthony Lake and Christine Todd Whitman, Chairs; Princeton N. Lyman and J. Stephen
Morrison, Project Directors
Independent Task Force Report No. 56 (2006)

In the Wake of War: Improving Post-Conflict Capabilities
Samuel R. Berger and Brent Scowcroft, Chairs; William L. Nash, Project Director; Mona K.
Sutphen, Deputy Director
Independent Task Force Report No. 55 (2005)

In Support of Arab Democracy: Why and How
Madeleine K. Albright and Vin Weber, Chairs; Steven A. Cook, Project Director
Independent Task Force Report No. 54 (2005)

Building a North American Community
John P. Manley, Pedro Aspe, and William F. Weld, Chairs; Thomas d'Aquino, Andrés
Rozental, and Robert Pastor, Vice Chairs; Chappell H. Lawson, Project Director
Independent Task Force Report No. 53 (2005)

Iran: Time for a New Approach
Zbigniew Brzezinski and Robert M. Gates, Chairs; Suzanne Maloney, Project Director
Independent Task Force Report No. 52 (2004)

An Update on the Global Campaign Against Terrorist Financing
Maurice R. Greenberg, Chair; William F. Wechsler and Lee S. Wolosky, Project Directors
Independent Task Force Report No. 40B (Web-only release, 2004)

Renewing the Atlantic Partnership
Henry A. Kissinger and Lawrence H. Summers, Chairs; Charles A. Kupchan, Project Director
Independent Task Force Report No. 51 (2004)

Iraq: One Year After
Thomas R. Pickering and James R. Schlesinger, Chairs; Eric P. Schwartz, Project Consultant
Independent Task Force Report No. 43C (Web-only release, 2004)

Nonlethal Weapons and Capabilities
Paul X. Kelley and Graham Allison, Chairs; Richard L. Garwin, Project Director
Independent Task Force Report No. 50 (2004)

New Priorities in South Asia: U.S. Policy Toward India, Pakistan, and Afghanistan
(Chairmen's Report)
Marshall Bouton, Nicholas Platt, and Frank G. Wisner, Chairs; Dennis Kux and Mahnaz
Ispahani, Project Directors
Independent Task Force Report No. 49 (2003)
Cosponsored with the Asia Society

Finding America's Voice: A Strategy for Reinvigorating U.S. Public Diplomacy
Peter G. Peterson, Chair; Kathy Bloomgarden, Henry Grunwald, David E. Morey, and
Shibley Telhami, Working Committee Chairs; Jennifer Sieg, Project Director; Sharon
Herbstman, Project Coordinator
Independent Task Force Report No. 48 (2003)

Emergency Responders: Drastically Underfunded, Dangerously Unprepared
Warren B. Rudman, Chair; Richard A. Clarke, Senior Adviser; Jamie F. Metzl,
Project Director
Independent Task Force Report No. 47 (2003)

Iraq: The Day After (Chairs' Update)
Thomas R. Pickering and James R. Schlesinger, Chairs; Eric P. Schwartz, Project Director
Independent Task Force Report No. 43B (Web-only release, 2003)

Burma: Time for Change
Mathea Falco, Chair
Independent Task Force Report No. 46 (2003)

Afghanistan: Are We Losing the Peace?
Marshall Bouton, Nicholas Platt, and Frank G. Wisner, Chairs; Dennis Kux and Mahnaz
Ispahani, Project Directors
Chairman's Report of an Independent Task Force (2003)
Cosponsored with the Asia Society

Meeting the North Korean Nuclear Challenge
Morton I. Abramowitz and James T. Laney, Chairs; Eric Heginbotham, Project Director
Independent Task Force Report No. 45 (2003)

Chinese Military Power
Harold Brown, Chair; Joseph W. Prueher, Vice Chair; Adam Segal, Project Director
Independent Task Force Report No. 44 (2003)

Iraq: The Day After
Thomas R. Pickering and James R. Schlesinger, Chairs; Eric P. Schwartz, Project Director
Independent Task Force Report No. 43 (2003)

Threats to Democracy: Prevention and Response
Madeleine K. Albright and Bronislaw Geremek, Chairs; Morton H. Halperin, Director;
Elizabeth Frawley Bagley, Associate Director
Independent Task Force Report No. 42 (2002)

America—Still Unprepared, Still in Danger
Gary Hart and Warren B. Rudman, Chairs; Stephen E. Flynn, Project Director
Independent Task Force Report No. 41 (2002)

Terrorist Financing
Maurice R. Greenberg, Chair; William F. Wechsler and Lee S. Wolosky, Project Directors
Independent Task Force Report No. 40 (2002)

Enhancing U.S. Leadership at the United Nations
David Dreier and Lee H. Hamilton, Chairs; Lee Feinstein and Adrian Karatnycky, Project
Directors
Independent Task Force Report No. 39 (2002)
Cosponsored with Freedom House

Improving the U.S. Public Diplomacy Campaign in the War Against Terrorism
Carla A. Hills and Richard C. Holbrooke, Chairs; Charles G. Boyd, Project Director
Independent Task Force Report No. 38 (Web-only release, 2001)

Building Support for More Open Trade
Kenneth M. Duberstein and Robert E. Rubin, Chairs; Timothy F. Geithner, Project Director;
Daniel R. Lucich, Deputy Project Director
Independent Task Force Report No. 37 (2001)

Beginning the Journey: China, the United States, and the WTO
Robert D. Hormats, Chair; Elizabeth Economy and Kevin Nealer, Project Directors
Independent Task Force Report No. 36 (2001)

Strategic Energy Policy Update
Edward L. Morse, Chair; Amy Myers Jaffe, Project Director
Independent Task Force Report No. 33B (2001)
Cosponsored with the James A. Baker III Institute for Public Policy of Rice University

Testing North Korea: The Next Stage in U.S. and ROK Policy
Morton I. Abramowitz and James T. Laney, Chairs; Robert A. Manning, Project Director
Independent Task Force Report No. 35 (2001)

The United States and Southeast Asia: A Policy Agenda for the New Administration
J. Robert Kerrey, Chair; Robert A. Manning, Project Director
Independent Task Force Report No. 34 (2001)

Strategic Energy Policy: Challenges for the 21st Century
Edward L. Morse, Chair; Amy Myers Jaffe, Project Director
Independent Task Force Report No. 33 (2001)
Cosponsored with the James A. Baker III Institute for Public Policy of Rice University

A Letter to the President and a Memorandum on U.S. Policy Toward Brazil
Stephen Robert, Chair; Kenneth Maxwell, Project Director
Independent Task Force Report No. 32 (2001)

State Department Reform
Frank C. Carlucci, Chair; Ian J. Brzezinski, Project Coordinator
Independent Task Force Report No. 31 (2001)
Cosponsored with the Center for Strategic and International Studies

U.S.-Cuban Relations in the 21st Century: A Follow-on Report
Bernard W. Aronson and William D. Rogers, Chairs; Julia Sweig and Walter Mead, Project Directors
Independent Task Force Report No. 30 (2000)

Toward Greater Peace and Security in Colombia: Forging a Constructive U.S. Policy
Bob Graham and Brent Scowcroft, Chairs; Michael Shifter, Project Director
Independent Task Force Report No. 29 (2000)
Cosponsored with the Inter-American Dialogue

Future Directions for U.S. Economic Policy Toward Japan
Laura D'Andrea Tyson, Chair; M. Diana Helweg Newton, Project Director
Independent Task Force Report No. 28 (2000)

First Steps Toward a Constructive U.S. Policy in Colombia
Bob Graham and Brent Scowcroft, Chairs; Michael Shifter, Project Director
Interim Report (2000)
Cosponsored with the Inter-American Dialogue

Promoting Sustainable Economies in the Balkans
Steven Rattner, Chair; Michael B.G. Froman, Project Director
Independent Task Force Report No. 27 (2000)

Non-Lethal Technologies: Progress and Prospects
Richard L. Garwin, Chair; W. Montague Winfield, Project Director
Independent Task Force Report No. 26 (1999)

Safeguarding Prosperity in a Global Financial System:
The Future International Financial Architecture
Carla A. Hills and Peter G. Peterson, Chairs; Morris Goldstein, Project Director
Independent Task Force Report No. 25 (1999)
Cosponsored with the International Institute for Economics

U.S. Policy Toward North Korea: Next Steps
Morton I. Abramowitz and James T. Laney, Chairs; Michael J. Green, Project Director
Independent Task Force Report No. 24 (1999)

Reconstructing the Balkans
Morton I. Abramowitz and Albert Fishlow, Chairs; Charles A. Kupchan, Project Director
Independent Task Force Report No. 23 (Web-only release, 1999)

Strengthening Palestinian Public Institutions
Michel Rocard, Chair; Henry Siegman, Project Director; Yezid Sayigh and Khalil Shikaki,
Principal Authors
Independent Task Force Report No. 22 (1999)

U.S. Policy Toward Northeastern Europe
Zbigniew Brzezinski, Chair; F. Stephen Larrabee, Project Director
Independent Task Force Report No. 21 (1999)

The Future of Transatlantic Relations
Robert D. Blackwill, Chair and Project Director
Independent Task Force Report No. 20 (1999)

U.S.-Cuban Relations in the 21st Century
Bernard W. Aronson and William D. Rogers, Chairs; Walter Russell Mead, Project Director
Independent Task Force Report No. 19 (1999)

After the Tests: U.S. Policy Toward India and Pakistan
Richard N. Haass and Morton H. Halperin, Chairs
Independent Task Force Report No. 18 (1998)
Cosponsored with the Brookings Institution

Managing Change on the Korean Peninsula
Morton I. Abramowitz and James T. Laney, Chairs; Michael J. Green, Project Director
Independent Task Force Report No. 17 (1998)

Promoting U.S. Economic Relations with Africa
Peggy Dulany and Frank Savage, Chairs; Salih Booker, Project Director
Independent Task Force Report No. 16 (1998)

U.S. Middle East Policy and the Peace Process
Henry Siegman, Project Coordinator
Independent Task Force Report No. 15 (1997)

Differentiated Containment: U.S. Policy Toward Iran and Iraq
Zbigniew Brzezinski and Brent Scowcroft, Chairs; Richard W. Murphy, Project Director
Independent Task Force Report No. 14 (1997)

Russia, Its Neighbors, and an Enlarging NATO
Richard G. Lugar, Chair; Victoria Nuland, Project Director
Independent Task Force Report No. 13 (1997)

Rethinking International Drug Control: New Directions for U.S. Policy
Mathea Falco, Chair
Independent Task Force Report No. 12 (1997)

Financing America's Leadership: Protecting American Interests and Promoting American Values
Mickey Edwards and Stephen J. Solarz, Chairs; Morton H. Halperin, Lawrence J. Korb, and Richard M. Moose, Project Directors
Independent Task Force Report No. 11 (1997)
Cosponsored with the Brookings Institution

A New U.S. Policy Toward India and Pakistan
Richard N. Haass, Chair; Gideon Rose, Project Director
Independent Task Force Report No. 10 (1997)

Arms Control and the U.S.-Russian Relationship
Robert D. Blackwill, Chair and Author; Keith W. Dayton, Project Director
Independent Task Force Report No. 9 (1996)
Cosponsored with the Nixon Center for Peace and Freedom

American National Interest and the United Nations
George Soros, Chair
Independent Task Force Report No. 8 (1996)

Making Intelligence Smarter: The Future of U.S. Intelligence
Maurice R. Greenberg, Chair; Richard N. Haass, Project Director
Independent Task Force Report No. 7 (1996)

Lessons of the Mexican Peso Crisis
John C. Whitehead, Chair; Marie-Josée Kravis, Project Director
Independent Task Force Report No. 6 (1996)

Managing the Taiwan Issue: Key Is Better U.S. Relations with China
Stephen Friedman, Chair; Elizabeth Economy, Project Director
Independent Task Force Report No. 5 (1995)

Non-Lethal Technologies: Military Options and Implications
Malcolm H. Wiener, Chair
Independent Task Force Report No. 4 (1995)

Should NATO Expand?
Harold Brown, Chair; Charles A. Kupchan, Project Director
Independent Task Force Report No. 3 (1995)

Success or Sellout? The U.S.-North Korean Nuclear Accord
Kyung Won Kim and Nicholas Platt, Chairs; Richard N. Haass, Project Director
Independent Task Force Report No. 2 (1995)
Cosponsored with the Seoul Forum for International Affairs

Nuclear Proliferation: Confronting the New Challenges
Stephen J. Hadley, Chair; Mitchell B. Reiss, Project Director
Independent Task Force Report No. 1 (1995)

Note: Task Force reports are available for download from CFR's website, www.cfr.org.
For more information, email publications@cfr.org.